The
Destructive
Element

The Destructive Element

New and Selected Poems

TURNER CASSITY

OHIO UNIVERSITY PRESS / ATHENS

Ohio University Press, Athens, Ohio 45701
© 1998 by Turner Cassity
Printed in the United States of America
All rights reserved

Ohio University Press books are printed on acid-free paper ⊚ ™

02 01 00 99 98   5 4 3 2 1

BT 1595 Net 5/98

Library of Congress Cataloging-in-Publication Data
Cassity, Turner.
    The destructive element : new and selected poems / Turner Cassity.
        p.   cm.
    Includes bibliographical referecnes (p.   ).
    ISBN 0-8214-1221-3 (cloth : alk. paper). — ISBN 0-8214-1222-1
(pbk. : alk. paper)
    I. Title.
  PS3553.A8D47   1998
  811'.54—dc21   97-37649
                                                            CIP

Acknowledgments

Some of the poems printed here appeared previously in the following collections.

Watchboy, What of the Night? Wesleyan University Press, 1966.

Steeplejacks in Babel. David R. Godine, 1973.

Yellow for Peril, Black for Beautiful. George Braziller, 1975.

The Defense of the Sugar Islands: A Recruiting Poster. Symposium Press, 1979.

Keys to Mayerling. R. L. Barth, 1983.

Hurricane Lamp. University of Chicago Press, 1986.

Lessons. R. L. Barth, 1987.

Mainstreaming: Poems of Military Life, by Turner Cassity, R. L. Barth, Warren Hope. R. L. Barth, 1987.

The Music of His History: Poems for Charles Gullans on His Sixtieth Birthday, ed. by Timothy Steele. R. L. Barth, 1989.

Between the Chains. University of Chicago Press, 1991.

Some of the poems in this collection initially appeared in the following periodicals: *Poetry, Southern Review, Chicago Review, North American Review, Poem, Yale Review, Quince, Emory University Quarterly, DeKalb Literary Arts Journal, Counter Measures, Denver Quarterly, Foxfire, Southern Poetry Review, Local Storms, Cumberland Poetry Review, Greensboro Review, Roberson Poetry Annual, Parnassus, Drastic Measures, Fontana, Sequoia, The Formalist, Ploughshares, Iowa Review, Renaissance, Poetry Miscellany, Lullwater Review, Chattahoochee Review, Michigan Quarterly Review, Shenandoah, Atlanta Review, Massachusetts Review, Edge City Review.*

Contents

From *Watchboy, What of the Night?* (1966)

From *Yellow for Peril, Black for Beautiful* (*1975*)

From *The Defense of the Sugar Islands: A Recruiting Poster* (*1979*)

From *Keys to Mayerling* (*1983*)

Imaginary Sargents (*1983*)

From *Hurricane Lamp* (1986)

From *Between the Chains* (*1991*)

The
Destructive
Element

Inward Turned, Outward Bound: New Poems

At the Palace of Fine Arts

In twelve-inch trophies for the champions
Of high school track teams, and in top awards
For Duplicate Bridge duos, Beaux-Arts live.
One would not offer to jeunesse dorée
Abstractions, or, to earnest experts, Pop.
The gilded statuettes—tiptoeing Wasps—
In their small way speak to the strong appeal
Of classic values: skill, proportion, fact.
If some cosmetic sexiness is there
That does no harm, of course. Could anyone
Except Rock Groups find sex in Henry Moore?
And if the hint of going through the motions
Chills, well, Duplicate by aim is that.
Generic athlete on your classic base
Of plinth and cornice, shaft and capital,
For what these were and can be, look around.
In this immense, expensive reconstruction
Of a building meant to look a ruin
Waits more life than fuels tournaments.
Its only problem is, what maintenance
Allot to monuments that honor wreck?
You, golden youth of what accomplishment,
Have too that problem. You will not be always
Equal to gilt and tiptoe. Think, therefore,
Yours is the ease of working by the rules;
And if you age, your ruin means. It may
Not; still, you will not then debase your base.
Contract redoubled, laurel wholly earned,
You enter the tradition; in that fire are burned.

Monumental Is More than a Question of Scale

Magnificently sited, on the choicest real estate,
The Soviet war monuments weight Central Europe down:
Les Beaux-Arts bloated. Buda must endure, on Gellert Hill,
A giantess who holds aloft a palm leaf. Fatally
For anything but levity, it looks much like a fish—
Mullet or salmon, say—and she a fishwife. Pest, too flat
To be a pedestal, escapes, but in the afternoon
Is in the shadow of that figure. Bratislava (Press-
burg, if you come by Autobahn) has its memorial
As floodlit focus for an avenue of cypresses.
A marble kiosk as discreet as Speer Berlin ignores;
Vienna screens a Worker Militant in fountain jets.
USSR does better for itself. In Volgagrad,
Colossal, in a strictest sense, the sword-uplifting *Rus*
Defends and is the Motherland; and in Odessa, plain,
Remote, an obelisk of dark red granite claims a shore,
Commemorating who knows what. The possibilities,
The Ukraine being what it is, are numberless and grim.
In ten more years, or twenty, will these tries, obtrusive now,
Become invisible as Sherman on Fifth Avenue,
Or have the force of Liberty Enlightening the World?
Remember Liberty was meant to honor Robespierre,
Not Ellis Island. If today it credits anyone
It's Gustave Eiffel, who contrived her brilliant skeleton.
And, I remind you, it's the dead of whom the figures speak.
The huddled masses in the ageless European snow,
American and German, Russian, Czech, Hungarian,
Now neither yearn nor breathe, nor know if they are tired or poor.
Already it is as if all the sites had shrunk to one,
Yet as effective it as any since the stone was rolled
And openness itself was tribute to an Easter morning.
Gateway also, classic, broad, and free, but whose whole fame

Once symbolized a wall, the resurrection secular
Transforms it in our very eyes to its own offering.
Its previous associations are not fortunate:
They vanish as the floodlights sweep the youth who line the top.
No better end than this: champagne on high in raw young hands;
The stones their fathers' hands laid down; replacement linden trees.

Meaner than a Junkyard Dog,
or,
Turner's Evil Twin

Our genes have junk in them. Not all the messages
That DNA contains does RNA read out.
Inheritance has drastic editing. What, though,
Are unused possibilities the relic of?
A better us, or worse? Are we as we exist
Young Dr. Jekyll failed or full-blown Hyde avoided?
(If avoided.) As of now we cannot know.
All we can say is, both the shadow archetype
And Doppelgänger, and the succubus as well,
Hang near us. Life, genetic outcome of a code
That has its blind spots, parallels what it is not—
An endless replicase of what it has destroyed
To be. Dumb corpse one carries, Siamese dark self
Whose only life is to embarrass, in our joint
Past where did we in aim diverge? Is it that aim
Was in itself the agency of difference?
Ambition's never quite evaded progeny,
A shadow is by definition follower.
But in the hidden mirror of the goal suppressed,
What proud construct of junk discarded bides his time?

Man of the Century

Gavrilo Princip

His portrait will not grace news magazines,
This killer of the morganatic wife
(I write here as a quasi-feminist)
And of her Archduke spouse, but by the bridge
In Sarajevo—it is named for him—
Each shell that falls is warhead to his shot,
As in Hiroshima (iambic, please)
His is the gesture of the blackened hand,
And Hiroshima (trochees now; I write
As a revisionist) itself much more
A monument to him than any bridge:
An ultimate in deconstructionism,
Somme—summation—of a quicker age.
Is it a worldwide cautionary tale
For freedom fighters, or below the Arch
Of Triumph of their sky eternal flame?
Historians cannot bend theory
To bend two ways at once. It's either/or.
The Dual Monarchy was born to flex;
And K.u.K. not being K.K.K.,
It did not lynch. It did not even hang.
Tuberculosis was, as one might say,
As Ruby to the Oswald, and it killed
After a Texas-brief captivity.
Free finally of some demented heir's
Blood-letting, foul, deformed longevity,
The last of 1914 cashes out,
Bankrupt, in Red Square fast food restaurants
And in the unity of one Berlin.
It is reborn in Herzegovina.
If ever there was Pilate's hour, pray, *Time*,
That it will strike again, to spare one here
Self-serving half-turns of the Rabbinate,
The all-destructive hot blood of the just.

Across the River and into the Sleaze

Across the river, or the county line,
Or just outside the city limits, or—
Juarez and Matamoros—out of reach
In Mexico, Sin City takes its ease:
A mockery of planned communities,
The city beautiful, greenbelts, Our Town,
Park cities, biosphere, the Habitat.
It is the triumph of the frontage road,
An ozone hole its bright Tiepolo.
Before we damn it as unnatural
We might do well to bear in mind asphalt
Is just as natural as grass. They both
Come up out of the ground. And as for vice . . .
It was a garden where the Fall took place.
The double serpent of the Interstate
Hangs high his lighted fruits on either side;
Their promise without season of a flesh
Always renewed. If ripeness is not all
It's more of it than greenness, and so too
Is rot. The porn-shop fronts are shining scales;
The two hides glitter at the outer edge
Of vision, saying each "Ye shall not eat?
Though every trace of passage will be shed?
Before the Garden is not of it, no?
I shall tout knowledge afterward as well.
There is a life outside of fruits and corn."
And Lilith's old ally is quite correct.
The secret of their Genesis success
Was saying Eden's was a hothouse air
And making God sound like a chaperon.
The truck-stops sparkle as the exit nears;
Now, forking neon spells out what we know.

In nature no abiding promise is,
Except of repetition, and—a truth
Of Lilith—at the end not even that.

The Glorified Go One by One to Glory

Follies of 2001

Before the century's oncoming end,
Or surely not long after, age unknown
From having been so many times writ false,
In wealth or poverty or mobile home
The last surviving Ziegfeld girl will die.
Of all who lined the ever-recurring stair
A final glory goes to what reward?
And, like a carpet when the bride has passed,
That time's grand staircase can be gathered up.
If in his will the bankrupt *Intendant*
Had funded, in the abstract, a reward
For this long tontine he could not foresee,
Would he have equaled in his fantasy
Such as the Girls attained to on their own:
San Simeon, Burke's peerage, *Modern Times*?
Is their extinction some in kind revenge
Of ostriches and egrets? Nakedness
Exacts its vengeance too. A skeleton
Is bare essentials bared. But let us bring,
As funeral directors bring dyed grass
To cemeteries, tread and riser back:
Folly in its root meaning is what fools
Accomplish, and there is no fool like a fool
Who thinks that he can turn back time. More reason,
Therefore, Folly's archetypal stair
Should share its image with the gold access
To Heaven and Eternity. Once more,
Paulette, Lorraine, Mae, Gladys, Marion,
Descend on shining slipper to the lights
That separate you from the eager dark.
What comes down, Numbered Beauties, must go up.

The Pied Piper
Maxfield Parrish

The older children too are mesmerized,
And girls especially. They help along the younger,
But they follow.

It's they, perhaps, who, early socialized
As nurses, household drudges, leave their homes in anger.
Ugly fellow,

He the Piper, so the Siren Song,
A soft flute obbligato, cannot be alluring
In the sense

Seduction is. It is the righted wrong
That lures, the promise of a Gypsy ease enduring:
Indolence.

Into the cavern goes Big Sister, guide
And follower, old maid, who will emerge hereafter
In bright rags

As Tarot fortune-teller, telling wide
And far, in wisdom's lazy matriarchal laughter,
She who lags
Her Piper does not call the tune. She is its crafter.

The Power of Abstraction

How many victims have they claimed,
The North Pole and the South?
Not only are they nothing, named;
Such as they aren't, they each year wobble.
As ego trips of death
They make K2 seem worth the trouble.

Vainglorious, dog-loving Scott,
Too fine to use a whip
And dying in his trek on foot;
Precise, position-fudging Peary,
Too strict to man a ship,
So reputation-proud it's eerie.

Nor need the Inuit puff up.
They are those litigants
That on pack ice attempt to map
Firm ground for future tribal hunting
(Or U.S. Air Base rents).
In spite of melt? Of ice floes shunting?

And we ourselves, as tourists, go,
As if it were a shrine,
To Nowhere in New Mexico,
Where it and Utah, Arizona,
Colorado join:
The drab Four Corner non-Sedona.

All you who follow in our track,
Do not lay out your all
On bare coordinates. Let crack
The whip and mush-off for a Klondike.

And having found it, wall
It off. Fortuna, dyke or non-dyke,

May comfort in Platonic cold,
Yet alter. If the Poles
Go round, can any fortune hold?
That pilgrimage around Polaris
So mocks, so dis-installs
The Absolute that where it tarries

Becomes not even place but guess.
If pilgrimage seems where
It's at, the Hadj be your success,
A First Crusade your crowning glory.
Mecca at least is *there;*
Jerusalem a more than story.

Making Orville's Day

Ikons begin somewhere, and if thereafter
They spread out, they do so by slow stages.
Lean Americans so lacking laughter
("When you say that, smile") at first are pages

Out of Owen Wister. Soon, however,
Word is flesh: the mute Wright Brother Wilbur.
Vizored cap, tight jacket lined in beaver,
Wilbur is his own Excalibur:

Rigidity defined. In picture-papers
Jaw and vizor set that knightly fashion
That will next appear, provoking vapors
At the matinée and the derision

Of the more articulate, as Gary
Cooper, who in turn is resurrected,
Taciturn as ever, in the wary,
Taut persona now Clint Eastwood. Acted

Out or driven in, what finds expression
In that effort not to laugh a little?
Fear that humor may outdraw ambition?
That one's missing tooth may let through spittle?

Is there, one must wonder, lost in Dayton
Some tradition counter? Rumor has it
Orville played those instruments of Satan
Mandolin and ukulele, facet

Of his genius too seldom thought of.
Neither brother got the girl, but filing
Lawsuits for a decade, Orville fought off
Pirates, making millions. He is smiling.

High Fashion

In its appearance tentative
As in performance, what we call,
In hope, the Shuttle, blazes off.

It may return. If it should not,
How name it? Probe? Projectile? Feint?
The triple rocket and the gross

Papoose it carries twist themselves
Out of the fire and into space:
Maneuver awkward as a dive

Run backward in a homemade film.
The cheapest studio would blush.
And, once deployed, the ugly shell,

Ceramic skin, seem out of place
As ever. Visibly, no thing
Can match the nothingness of space.

And in the lucent lower air,
Entirely of it, for it, shape
Accommodating, motion mated,

Tall hot-air balloons string pearl
Along the winds that they enclose,
Up-end pear ear-drops in the sky,

To be as fit a jewelry
As cold auroras, warmed how so
From their own body heat, propane.

It's "mode of transport," notice. "Mode."
As décor, science stands, dates, falls.
The burn that lifts was fossil laid.

Never Use a Stock Ticker
without a Geiger Counter

Far from Promontory—in a safe
In Palo Alto whose design, a sphere of sorts,
Its set of handles, porthole window of thick quartz,
Assure us 1869 could have

Stockpiled plutonium—the Golden Spike
Is on exhibit. Leland Stanford leave to Utes
And vandals twenty-five Troy ounces? It disputes
All probability. How very like

The Senator in one hand to have had
Sledge-hammer, and a crowbar in the other. That,
The Spike's discreet removal, we have neither plate
Nor tintype of. If to its scene I add

A Chinese laborer, dead buffalo,
Train smoke, transvestite shaman broken out in hives—
If not in smallpox—I've a Currier, an Ives
Some print collector would delight to show.

Oh. I forgot a proto-Harvey Girl,
The *Ur*-Leona Helmsley. Only in black chaps,
I mean, not starchy apron. Do forgive the lapse,
And my omission of the pristine curl

Of prairie grass reconstituted. Gold,
It is apparent at the luxury of distance,
Is both immense potential and a toxic substance,
As caution rightly treats it. Was the hold

The Son of Heaven had the simple force
Of yellow, as is too the writ of quarantine?
Chinamen have their chance, Utes pocks, and we vaccine.
To half-life all decays. Not gold of course.

The Blood of the Widow Oosthuizen*

It was at Sutter's Mill the sweating sun,
As at Langlaagte, high and waterless,
It was a shining silt, and in Peru
The bright toe-stubbing stone upon the veld.
Immobile in Fort Knox the shifting rates,
And in your hand the yellow burial.
It is, as I have shown you, pure exchange.
And, finally, it is itself: one bar
Whose weight would stagger any slave in Zurich,
Broker on the bourses in Ophir.
Now melting in its crucible of clay,
Above a cirque of gas jets, as its last
Impurities envelop it and burn,
Ayesha of the precious metals, gold
Alone goes in the flame, the blue renewal,
To end as more than ever what it was.
And being more than ever what we are,
We, as apparently we must, obey.

* Upon whose farm at Langlaagte in the Transvaal gold was discovered in 1886.

Soldiers of Orange

The highway outside Amsterdam picks up
That well known Dutch non-treat a frontage road,
Access to aging villa colonies
And partially successful restaurants
Carved out of them. The Tuans have their pick:
Indië, Soerakarta, Tanah Abang.
Near the last I jump the median,
U-turn, and park. I am to meet for lunch,
Eternities beyond my great escapes,
A Mrs. Yerger Wallace Lampton, whom,
As Ellen Dean, I almost married twice.

. . .

The dining room is soda fountain Conrad:
Beaded curtains by formica tables.
Ellen, in the caracul, red hair,
And strong Chanel of all those years ago,
Has with her Neill, her daughter, who wears shorts.
Worse still, she looks much like the Ur-LaNeill,
Her father's mother. God cannot be good.
"I know it's Howard Johnson," Ellen says,
"But both the cooks were on the Rotterdam.
I'm in my fur so you can't see the pounds
They add."
                    "A greasy chopstick," Neill complains.
"It means 'red dirt' in Javanese, or what.
One might as well be back in Mississippi."
"Yes. 'The immemorial red hills
Of Tanahabang County, where the scent
Of burning godowns moseys over weevil
At the root . . .' And speaking of prevailing,
How is Erg?"

"Full colonel, if you please,
And power mad. I know the sort of thing
Yvonne de Gaulle must go through. Hilversum,
Our base, is just a few miles down the road.
Maneuvers are in progress now, else Erg
Would be here with us. We shall have instead
The pleasure—brace yourself—of Emma Zander."
"No. How did you find her?"
                                    "Yerger did.
Her father's NATO for the Netherlands."
"A girl we used to know in high school, Neill."
"I've met her. Central High, to hear her talk,
Was quite the social climax of her life.
It tells us what to think of Hilversum."
"Queen Juliana's seamstress makes her dresses;
Otherwise she's as she was. Oh dear.
I think that we're involved in the Maneuvers."
Two small military vehicles
Pull up onto the Red Dirt's sandy lawn;
A group of men in red berets, silk scarves,
And, one can see, re-tailored uniforms
Dismount and demonstrate the S.O.P.
Of going through bead curtains soundlessly.
"G.I. mascara?" Neill suggests.
                                    "Tattoo
Would be the kind assumption, I believe."
"Tattoos don't run."
                    "Tattooing's Maori
In any case, not Indonesian," adds
The expert (the mascara expert: Ellen).
Bonelessly the Javanese conform
Their bodies to the chairs, and very soon
Are in some sort of contest to see which
Have fingers long enough to bend full back
And touch the wrist. "Limp-wristed! They're pure rubber,"
Ellen says, not unadmiringly.
Arthritis, as I know, breeds tolerance.

"What is the uniform?" I ask.
                              "It's Dutch;
I can't make out the shoulder patch from here."
"Well while you two infer I'm going to ask,"
Says Neill, and to the loud back-handed joy
Of the contestants, joins them at their table.

. . .

"When they found out I was double-jointed
They told all," says she on her return.
"They're medics, although with those fingernails
They must cause bleeding massive as they stop.
And we have much more life in Hilversum
Than we suspected. Every other week
Is Balinese folk-dancing night. So far
As I can figure out this all takes place
In some friend's B.O.Q. They each have friends."
"It's 'friends' who got them out in '47."
"Rankers," Ellen shudders. "They let rankers
In the B.O.Q.? For Heaven's sake
Don't let your father know. He's sure the Dutch
Vote Left already." Her priorities,
I see, are in that order I remember.
At the door a clattering of beads
Distracts us. Emma Zander, in a dress
Of muscadine and scuppernong brocade,
Is tangled in the curtain. "Wilhelmina
Drag," assesses Neill. For all her joints,
She is her mother's child. The curtain rod
Has settled onto Emma's shoulders. Not
Oranje but the Princess Turandot,
And who would risk his head for Emma Zander?
Chivalry, however, is not dead.
The medics rise and free her, bead by bead.
But then, to paraphrase, their name is love.

. . .

The highway outside New Iberia
Is pure Louisiana. Causeway, culverts,
Low roadhouses raised on cypress pilings.
Names, however, are not quite the ones
That I recall. We have now Indochine,
Mekong, the Hue. As I could document
From photographs, the last was, at one time,
The Huey Long Bait Shack. The new regime
Has simply sawed away such of the sign
As was not relevant. There is no need
To be surprised. Here French is spoken; fish
Is eaten; rice is grown. An Indochine-
Louisiane menu can hardly fail,
But I have reasons not to stop and eat.
In New Iberia, alike divorced,
Are Ellen and the other daughter, Reeve.
Each has become that grim phenomenon
A woman going down a list. I speed,
Until I realize the State Patrol
Has choppers overhead. And as the blades
Of shadow sweep my windshield, I can see,
A summer re-run of a summer scene,
The telecasts of Saigon at the end.
I see the fire, the Embassy Compound,
The airlift: endless hands that seem to stretch,
Like rubber, toward the ropes, and toward these signs.
If I should pull in at the Cafe Nam,
What scene would I encounter? Friends of friends?
A wave of swamp-flies spatters on my hood.
We should defoliate Louisiana.

Outward Bound

In mid-October, 1929,
The *Berengaria*, Cunard's ex-German
Flagship, is at sea. A stock exchange
On board, a Wall Street on an upper deck,
Ticks-in the dropping figures of the Crash:
An abstract iceberg, quick torpedo-hit.
The sea-bourse closes as the trading day
Completes; the Smoking Room is full till dawn.
A First Class less first class will disembark
To what New York they do not know. Mid-ocean,
No one changes to a cheaper cabin;
None fails to sign a chit, none, just yet, jumps.

December 5th of 1941
Is on a Friday. In a white and purple
Blaze of orchids and a wash of rum
The Matson Steamship *Lurline*, from a dazed
Aloha Tower, sails for San Francisco.
Sunday . . . lots of people sleep on deck.
Radio silence, blackout. On the Coast
The guessing is, the ship is sunk. As Act
Of God loopholes are shamelessly invoked
By underwriters and as greedy heirs
Begin to probate wills, the shaken ship
Triumphantly puts-in the Golden Gate.
The last elite beachcombers go ashore.

What is it to embark in one decade
And come home to another? Hastened age?
Are there time-warps if they are not perceived?
Who, on the other hand, could miss a rain
Of brokers or those long detention trains

Of Japanese? In transit eat your meals;
They have been paid for. Save the ticker tape.
Confetti may be hard to come by. Tip.
The stewards may be revolutionaries.
Practice language. It is all you have.
Heirs? Do not trust them. Sign each codicil.

Rondo on the Rio Negro

> Having fallen on bad times, Manaus is now experiencing a
> second boom, thanks to its free port status, declared in
> 1967, and a growing electronics industry, under Japanese
> patents.
>
> —*Manaus, a Tourist Guide*

Manaus at the floating dock
Is all the seasons' water-clock

And every seller's flood gauge. Just
How high the wet goes up the rust

Is how much space a vendor gets
For peppers, suckling pigs, and pets

Along the foreshore. Opposite,
Four miles away and out of sight,

The other shores, as floods impact,
Express a balance as exact:

High water routs as many lives
As commerce. Always, rain arrives;

Cycles are cycles. On the bluff,
Fragmenting, but restored enough,

The wrought-iron of the rubber boom,
Encompassed by the twining gloom

From every vine that science knows,
Survives into these concrete rows

Of worker housing for the rich.
For now, a Sony is both itch

And its appeasement. Ease, theft, flair . . .
Japan is what the barons were,

If subtler in its labor sweeps.
The gashed wild rubber, though, still weeps,

Although its gatherers today
Are by and large the déclassé

Gone native. Foremen decades since,
White, half-breed, nine-tailed into mince

True Indians. In latex camps
Of green and complicated damps

The last of 1910 drips on.
If others covet silicon

Perhaps its chips, like rubber seed,
Someone can smuggle out and breed.

The free port will be rusting sheds;
The free go back to shrinking heads.

Double Passage on the Holland-Amerika

Designed for long North River piers and not for cruising,
Nieuw Amsterdam takes up the dockside in San Juan.
And, as the crew comes off, it out-exotics it.
In 1954 no one, and least of all
The Netherlands, will own to hiring lascars. Not
Sumatrans? Dyaks? Javanese? The officers
Who tally-off the tourists are so spic and blond
They would be tarred as raving High Colonials—
Tar being white as well as black—if they were each
Precursors of a Peace Corps acting Gandhi out,
Or Angels of the Lord come down dispensing cures.
I am a young man in the Army reading Conrad;
It's almost more than I can stand: the full effect
Of earrings and of fish-heads, and of Tuan Jim
Before the fall, in the enjoyments of a weekend pass.

In 1992 I am as old as Marlow.
Not to brag, almost as traveled. On a warm
Fall day in San Francisco, near as memory,
Nieuw Amsterdam sails in. Another of that name;
Lord Jim's command is long since in the wreckers' hands.
But as if answering a summons, here I am,
Again beside the pier. If who sought after youth
And fountain did not find them, it is possibly
Because it never dawned on them to ask in Dutch,
Or check the bilges. And as into Miramar
So long ago, the men head for their own time off.
They have had orthodontia, or a better diet—
All the fish, not just the head. The summer whites
Set off the half-caste, as the deep suntans the blond.
Must I re-read *An Outcast of the Islands,* or re-write it?

Tulips from Alcibiades

Having at one time no ecology,
Or partisan for its ecology,
The Zuider Zee is dammed about and drained.
And of its shallow waters comes, in time,
A landscape of another planet: God
Improved upon. Hydraulic engineers,
And social, create Eden as a grid.
Unnatural, but as the saying goes,
The Dutch upon the Eighth Day made the land
Themselves. And in the center they have placed,
As in the Garden was the focal Tree,
A model village. Serpentless the seed
Of Adam leach out of the sand the salt;
And do not know, or seem to know, the more
That they obey the more the limits press.
It does not flame, but in the guarding hands
Of civil servants land use is a sword.
Across the dikes, along the former shore,
Are courage, knowledge, and the mark of Cain.
In their own time they will admit themselves,
As once the sea wormed in. One does not match
An adolescent Dutch Boy with an asp,
Or if one does, sends out a mongoose too.
It is the least the Indies can return:
Out there is venom, land, and land to spare.
A polder, perfect in its flatness, trim,
May seem a plain as a platonic form,
But it's a plain. Its ideal villages
Will show us soon enough they are the cities.

Kurt Weill in Curaçao

The gables are not Dutch so much as they are Herbert Baker:
Cape Town in the Caribbean; and the postcard faker

Touches out the *most* unwindmill-like smokestacks and smoke
Of Shell's immense refinery, itself OPEC baroque.

A Juliana Bridge and Wilhelmina statue, earning
Pride of place, invoke another sort of home fires burning,

And pre-Manhattan Peter Stuyvesant, peg-leg and all,
As onetime governor, has also pride of pedestal.

Perhaps the ultimate of Dutch, the Cafe Surabaya.
Does it serve good rijsttafel? *Had Maria Ouspenskaya*

Wrinkles? At the bar, a question and the quick response
Are not, but might well be, a late transplanted Afrikaans.

Not knowing Papiamento, it is Afrikaans I'll quote.
"Ag, Janie! Ek het guilders. Het jy tyd?" I'll not footnote,

But as a hint I'll tell you that when May comes on whenever,
It is September that will end up buying the Genever.

"Jy het nie hart nie, Janie." But the tropics have no seasons,
And hearts that have no heart have guilders, Peter, for their reasons.

Two Sides of the Mackie Messer Mouth

in memory of Dean Greenough,
1961–1992

In other days, and easier,
He would have been an unremarkable,
Though most intelligent young man.

In prospects ever queasier,
Without real self-deceit, already ill,
He did, completely, what one can:

Informed himself, so his each choice
Was sound, although he fully realized
One has to choose beneath the knife;

Spoke up in a courageous voice
Against contempt; gazetted, organized;
Saw to it that he had a life.

And when he knew that he would die,
Or, worse, go blind, he simply chose to do
What he had done: know, live, choose, see.

He did not use the word, but I . . .
I do; and though I've done some knifing too,
I turn my tongue to say to you
How he was brave. He had to be.

The Mount of the Holy Cross

Rumors of its existence being old,
The Spanish priests in Colorado must,
Undoubtedly, have seen it. Indians
Cannot have made much of it. Cross, for them,
Would not have signaled *in hoc signo*. Let
Full credit for discovery redound
On that itinerant photographer.
Who, mule for darkroom, made his freakish mount
(The Mountain, I refer to, not the mule)
A natural for calendars back East.
Longfellow's "Cross of Snow," a calendar
Art versified, was more publicity.
By 1929 a president,
Ex-miner Herbert Hoover, on the strength,
One must imagine, of the photographs,
The Mountain being inaccessible
As ever, had that snow in the crevasse
Proclaimed, as Mountain of the Holy Cross
National Monument. His interest,
Of course, could have been geological.
If the Depression had not intervened,
Would there have been a cog railroad? Pastel
Floodlights, and choirs, as at Niagara?
A little more lead time, a local P.
T. Barnum, and the 19th century,
Not ever one to do a thing by halves,
Would profitably have had a Passion Play;
Or at the least, projecting on the cross
The Body and the Blood, a lantern-slide
Originating at the largest lamp
And lens yet manufactured: opticals
Paid for by Sunday Schools, Light of the World

Lighthouse as a projection booth.

                             Meanwhile,

One arm has melted. Long dry summers. Dust
Bowl decades. Quietly, the Monument
Is de-gazetted, heading off conflict
Of Church and State, or the suggestion He
Who hung between two thieves might have Himself
Been something of a one-armed bandit. God
Has dried away the problem which He put.
Or has He? Snow that in the Great Salt Lake
Has inundated dance pavilions has,
Upon the peak at Leadville, nailed again
The full crossarm and thousand-foot upright.
A chair lift might exploit it. Postcards show,
Already, colored helicopter views.
It is the merest tic of time before
Evel Knievel, say, decides to ski
From wound to wound, or, every Saturday,
Weekend stunt pilots write I.N.R.I.
Will militant agnostics bring napalm?
Embarrassing, to have the problem back.
If, nearer to it, in a scent of pines,
Golgotha is a hasty crystal stream,
And summer lightning braids, if not a crown,
An earl's uneven coronet of thorn;
If when in campfire-light the dice are thrown
That symbol at the valley-head prevails,
It soon will be innocuous: a snow
In snow. Gazette it as an icy graph
That goes and comes: abcissa, ordinate—
Search, formula, mirage. For all we know
This lava pinnacle or that may be
Buddha as seen at Kamakura, Pan
In Kensington, or Gitchee Manitou.
Tomorrow, onto any canyonside,
A plane may crash and leave its skeleton

To be a burned-out tetragrammaton.
Dare one remind the Courts that Government
Has so far, acting through Space Agencies,
Expended millions on what, in this high
Clear night, is patently the Prophet's Crescent?

Horizons and Myopia

Blues going off to gray;
The wind that blows one way.

Highway without a bend;
Fences that never end.

Cornflowers, one or two;
Horizon near to view,

If just as fragment. Trees?
Intrusions. Let the breeze

Pass undeterred, abstract
As Central in the act

Of going Mountain. Set
Your clock. No need to fret.

Is there not time and time?
Although, in prospect, climb

To forests. Narrowings,
They. Trees and their tight rings

Say as by wooden lip
I've often made this trip.

Or would beneath the saw
(A suburb in the raw).

Meanwhile, the Tumbleweed
Mocks fixity, a deed,

Idea of real estate.
Between the Golden Gate

And here no survey holds.
No map but Air's unfolds.

Dead reptiles give it scale;
Cacti are it in Braille:

How I at blind three score
Trace every mile once more.

Number One Nob Hill

Hotel Mark Hopkins

The brick forecourt endures the morning shadow;
Floors above, its daylight broad, assured,
The giant flag streams out in wind from China—

Stripes and stars, and bluer, squarer sky:
As if the wind contained cosmogony.
As if that wind were light, and had for light years

Been in transit, so that on the staff
Are fixed the colors of a Treaty Port:
One mongrel banner, extraterritorial of time.

Enormous house flag of a house remote,
Enduring enclave, mandate won of Heaven,
On our highest roof confer your hope,

Your sometime trade whose sources now are dark.
Oahu learns all harbors soon are Pearl,
And on the flagpole here, for all I know,

The wind is artificial—tricks and jets,
Core hollow at the center of the steel.
A little compressed air, free trade, and God will save the Mark.

Un bel di vedremo

In afternoon the light streams in from Asia,
And in Japan Town, in the closed-in Trade Mall,
Making a minute but real occasion
Of what could have been a bit of treadmill,
The Bar Lounge Shinjuku at four o'clock reopens.
It is, for who are waiting, pretty much what happens.

Military, decades in retirement,
(Occupation Army, '47)
Occupying now a petty torment
Of the single life, or in-law coven.
Here, to an insistent slamming of the dice cups,
Is a fallout frozen as the polar ice caps.

Lacquer, scent, rice powder on the owner;
Ankle straps and open toes the footwear
For her helpers. In a chosen corner
Widows too wear what they on the boat wore.
Later, when the rival Nihon Machi closes,
The local Japanese themselves will find excuses,

Look, come in. All too easy to imagine,
In them one sees, in their cool self-containment,
How "diversity" turns state religion.
With that utter lack of all attunement
They might be British native to the Orange Free State.
Is it the exiled heirs who do not die intestate?

Once in years to Tokyo suffices;
Bloemfontein, once Union Castle folded,
Does not leave at all. It had its uses,
Shinjuku, but soon they will have yielded.
Mainstream beers Asahi and Kirin, Suntory
Any whisky. One fine day, One World, world-weary.

Ten on the Richter

Along the street like gaunt ex-sentinels,
Or, inappropriate, but truth will out,
Obese ex-sentinels, the hungry mount their guard.

One cannot call them homeless. From their Hell's
Half-Acre—half square yard—they put to rout
Intruders; territorial, and by it scarred.

Pursuing, then, the martial model, say
A sentry-box is how to help: half-height,
Half-heated; soup bowl; kitty-litter. It's a squat,

But it's an address, and a man's space, slot,
Whatever, is his castle. On the Right
We might take neo-Prussianism all the way

And from the sidewalk snatch off Dixie Cups
And woolen caps that hold their change and swap
For shakos, which hold more, and, further, stand up straight.

Costumers have them, in the style, one hopes,
That has an *ivoire* death-head at the top.
As mascot, HIV may up the giving rate.

In place already, programs of the Left
Support apparently some sort of fund
That has allowed one sentry lately to afford

Hair-dye and bottled water. But restored
Self-confidence is as it comes, and shunned
In time of drought, tap water is a form of theft.

If on the skids and on the skateboard tend,
In California, somewhat to merge,
The glaring common factor being toothlessness,

When social or the seismic truces end,
And martial law, soup kitchens, and the surge
Of virus come to all, is that a scaled redress,

Or acid rain upon the just, unjust,
And situation ethos? 1906
Had too its regimental watch, vain cheats, its ill,

Its little cooking fires; and one sees still
These one-man bivouacs beside the Styx.
Have we learned nothing? No, we've learned a rich distrust.

Philip the Fair on Folsom Street

Baphomet, idol of the Templars, waits as near
As any other god, as far outside of time.
His worshipers, therefore, array him as they wish:
Upon his metal skin lay ribbons of their flesh;
The pallor of his alloy color with their blood;
His all-demanding chill envelop in their sweat;
On nipples cut from opal—fire, I say, not milk—
In frenzy break their teeth; in their own foreheads, minds
As well? carve out the hole his jewel caste-mark fits.
To replicate an ikon's silent lack of breath
A studded collar tightens; the adored club foot
Each honors in the cleated fall of heel on instep.
It is the pedal password of a wordless cult.
Between the mock-colossal legs, the distant stance
Of fallen Rhodes, in turn prostrate themselves
The innocent of Heraclitus, seeking still
To be wet twice by one stream never quite the same:
A plumber's David as the brimming mannikin,
Baphomet has had water laid, although of his
Proud body's fluids he demands no quick exchange.
He has it slowly, in the drip, the draining life
About him. Altars are not now a god's stone sling,
Or how so strong desire, bondage necessity.
The Temple's sacrifices walk, and Time has made
Of each a water-clock, a faulted vessel, dry
Already at the top and just enough aware
To count the seeping torture of their dwindling days.
The one capacity Baphomet does not have
Is site selection. He can only follow. First
Edessa and the provinces of Saladin;
Thereafter Acre, Cyprus, France. And now what is,
If it is nothing else—its suppurating back
Against the wall, proselytizing to the end,
Its leprosy its polity—a last Crusader State.

A Word from Isobel

The dilemma of her widowhood was whether or not to burn
Burton's translation of *The Perfumed Garden*, an ancient
Persian sex manual, along with his notes.

—*The Life of Sir Richard Francis Burton*

All that I burned I first had read;
Had read and understood. No dread

Of fact impelled me, or some fear
Of the obscene. Did I not steer

The *Nights* through publication? Rank—
And as such, money in the bank—

Rank as it is I could have done
The Perfumed Garden. And not one

Among you would have learned from it
What women know by mother wit.

Lovemaking learned from any book
Is castling with some other's rook.

So, all of you who mourn the loss,
Remember that the torch and toss

Were an informed decision. Pride,
Love, tact, and Church are on my side.

You have that prurience you slip
By in the guise of scholarship;

I have such garden as I find,
Perfumes of Hope, and peace of mind.

Astrology in the Sahara

Zagora

The low wind-devils whirl among the camelthorns,
And add their bit of desert to the failing field.
In motions of immense sidewinders, loose,
Relentless, quietly come in the dunes.
The barriers go under and the ditches fill;
In corrugated dust and mucous-stiffened eyes
Time's yellow death precedes itself. Are these
Such docile grains as in a sandglass wait
To measure desiccation on another scale?
As these long winds lay bare the jawbone of an ass
So too an hourglass may. The more that skulls
Appear—a goat, a fossil lion? ram—
The more we recognize a making zodiac.
Here is the archer's bow, if it is not the bow
Of some dead rebec player; here is too
(Oases are not far) the fish. Watch now
The water-bearer pass, the jug held shoulder high.
Doubt not the scorpion will find us in our sleep,
Or that the Faith sees to virginity.
We each are twin, if only good and bad:
What but a balance lacks? The crab may come. Hope, Twin,
That he is fossil. How the fatal trickle tells!
And how the captive sand we count has its revenge.

Oued Draa

A silted water by the towered towns,
So faint of impetus as to deny
High Atlas as a source, the River Draa
Sets eastward toward the mouth it does not have:
The desert where it wholly dries, or has
Some mythic after-presence underground—
A mummy of a river, or bequest,
Or dusty question on a doubtful map.
Its dead bulrushes follow it a while,
Then they too disappear. If caravans
Extend it by their ancient routes, the map
Denotes them by a line more space than ink,
And Earth denotes them not at all. Prayer—star—
The sun comes up along the parallel
Of Mecca. That too Earth and sand ignore,
Though where the surface of the mosque peels off
One sees the sun-dried brick have azimuth,
As in the covered markets, when the skeins
Are taken and the colors gathered in,
The dyers' emptied frameworks plot the dark.
Eternal snows bear up the sky behind;
Eternal equally, the sands before.
Our course between . . . Or does to call it course
Imply such plotting as it may not have?
It is decline that moves it, waste that ends.

Regression Analysis

Notice that Abraham, called on
To make a human sacrifice,
Knows just exactly what is done,
And demonstrates no great surprise;

As Isaac, like a prime Aztec,
Does not resist the lifted knife.
The firewood, gathered at the beck
And call of God, awaits the life

That dampens it, that it will dry.
Hard truth a teller softens, mutes.
Isaac is freed, but by and by.
No scholarship today disputes

That in the bold original
Red Riding Hood's grandmother *was*
The wolf. So fit the pieces all
Together, and you have good cause

To doubt that it was any ram
Obedience saw offered up.
"I am," One said once, "that I am."
Yet, in the telling, He's a group

Of Hebrew consonants. Is four;
No vowels. Guards his privacy,
Jehovah. Is it all the more
To have your heart out, Isaac? Say.

Walking on Water

There is no secret to it. Test the surface tension
First; place the foot. If currents run in opposition
Change direction. Where you end is not the point.

As in most miracles the eye of the beholder
Counts. Fishermen, who wade perforce in their profession,
Know mere wading, vintners watered wine. To feed

Five thousand does not much impress a caterer.
Raise up a dead embalmer if you wish to awe—
Those few who care to have him back. And bear in mind

Translation too is miracle. A walking by
Is not a walking on, and God is everywhere,
Not least, perhaps, in prepositions and their objects.

Sitting behind Ben-Hur

The drumbeat sets the oar-stroke, cruelly;
But then we do not choose our heartbeat.

Manacles confine us. Who, however,
Can be really said to venture?

If in the battle it is row or drown,
We row. The lash is often on us.

It is an incentive, in its way.
The rowing builds up shoulder muscles.

I've a tan. I look at backs a lot.
I deeply understand teamwork.

I live in filth. Was I fastidious
When I was free? Here sharks will have us;

It's not as though elsewhere there are not jackals.
Bear up. Hand and heart grow calloused.

Joshua Ben-Panthera

His enemies said that he was the son of a Roman soldier
named Panthera and a Galilean peasant woman.

—Morton Smith, *Jesus the Magician*

I was a soldier's son, and restless therefore.
My good stepfather's trade I did not care for,

Though I learned it. Carpentry is squaring,
Leveling. It has no room for daring.

My alarming cousin's headless crying
In the wilderness was more defying,

So I have this going fate of criers:
Questioning, raw back, a crown of briars.

What's ahead is woodwork pure and simple.
Crosspiece, upright. Deadwood from the Temple.

Christ of the Andes

More realistic than the airstream Christ
Above the Bay at Rio, Christus here,
As if He stepped out of a Zurbarán
Into a constant Force Six wind, allows
The loose bronze of His robe to billow. Placed
Exactly on the border as an end
To border wars, the statue mans the pass
Not as a symbol but as sentinel.
Above the timberline of wood for rood,
In thinner air than prayer can carry in,
At altitude beyond the reach of faith,
Its lilies in the breath of worshipers,
The staring image on its arid slope
Brings into mind embodied Easter less
Than Easter Island. Not incongruous,
Entirely, thought of distance and of surf,
And warring Polynesia's farthest reach;
Outrigger voyages and certain pots,
The stars as sure as any Magi had.
Who said to fishers "I shall make of you
Fishers of men," Whose Father worked in clay,
They neither of Them would have let it go
At that, aware sea-level fosters life,
And navigation brings in more than nets.

Christ of the Ozarks

So far below *Achttausender,* if far
Above the wedding chapels in the dells,
The hills provide a modest pedestal
For this assault on Him of Sunday School:
Some blind woodcarver's rigid toy grown tall,
A seven-story shaft of pseudo-Folk,
Unconscious hint of Jesus as a Golem,
Or pilot project for a windmill farm.
The features of the Hoffmann portrait may,
As has been said, suggest a bearded lady,
But do at least suggest a Word made flesh
Instead of made cartoon. Perhaps the face
Agreed on in Byzantium was best:
Full front, the forward stare that fixes, brow
Surround of measured punctures for the thorns,
And hair as if the Prophet's severed head,
Damp Ras Tafarian, rose off the salver.
Distant immensely from Veronica,
We live by image just as much as she,
Our minds imprinted by the sweats that pass
And burdens we are fated not to bear—
The veil's betraying need to visualize.
There is no certainty that what it lacks
Imagination can, convincingly,
Depict. A high priest of the Aztecs could,
No doubt more fully than Murillo, draw
The Sacred Heart. What distance gives us here
Is whittling, carpentry become a toy.

The Canals of Pera

The planet Pera orbits far beyond;
Beyond not only Pluto, but beyond
Whatever evidence there outside lies.
It is by definition other. Time
For it is not eternity for us;
It is eternal present: any tense
One longs for. Youth? Of course not. Middle age,
But middle age defended and enclosed,
Inside the rings and moons; an even plain
Triumphal incandescence arches over,
Rounded ice protects. If in its sky
Our broken past sweeps on in gaps and light,
Our future turns unbrokenly one face,
That too is other. In the sky of Earth
It is the past that never turns away
And gaps which are the future wholly: ring
Inscrutable, invisible, agape—
wide circle set to trap the animal
And with itself as bait; alluring void
Inhabitants of Pera need not seek,
Unthreatened on their plain outside of time,
Who look on youth as on a planet red,
Or as deep wounds in theirs, that never were.

I am no neo-Nazi. Nazi, maybe,
If my liking Albert Speer indicts me.
Say of me that I love to trace the AB
C of German-Greek. What so invites me

Is line: the seamless scale from classicism
To high Wilhelmine to the later eagles;
As if stone genes, or some automatism,
Were in fact controlling, and whose struggles

To survive, to go on uncontested,
Created at the end not frozen music
But frozen scores: an art two times arrested,
And, as structure, morally aphasic.

If buildings speak it is by way of echo.
That is as true of Second Empire gilding
As of benuded Mussolini Deco
Or U. of Moscow Early Woolworth Building

(Stalin Purgative). True too I like them.
I also like New Delhi Pukka Sahib.
If I address four walls—you may select them—
The style of which revisionists at rehab

Know as, in their chauvinistic manner,
International, the connotation
Will be what I read into them, planner
Notwithstanding: create uncreation.

Because Columbus House, designed by Erich
Mendelsohn, was used by the Gestapo

As a Berlin precinct, should the Zurich
Handelsbank not rent it? Let *Da Capo*

Set the moral standard and no mortar,
Banker, brick, or stone can go untainted,
Sin being our beginning. Court Recorder,
Can one white a sepulcher, then vaunt it?

Iconography

As idols go
The Feathered Serpent is the archetype:
Implacable,
Not warmth or aid,
Totemic closeness, mascot; not a charm.

Beside that stair
He parallels he waits the sacrifice:
The chosen heart
Provided all
And fattened on three hundred days: fit gift

To one for whom
The deer and maize can never be enough.
To who is brought
He nods no sign.
He does not promise. He is both the fang

And quetzal, tight
Embrace, or doubting tongue that distances,
Who is himself
The self-renewed—
The knowing god emergent, past put by.

Ourselves a skin
We cannot shed, a blood we cannot cool,
We meet his eye.
Who stares down whom?
Is subtlety much ward against a pulse

Which mounts to heights
Of no returning, having all to lose?

Give in to glut,
Give in to love,
And as we pass give back the snake his spit.

The Custom of the Country

Into the Well of Sacrifice warm flesh a priesthood throws.
Around, around she goes; where she comes out, nobody knows.

What *is* known is that such a sacrifice puts off the need
For calendar reform. It times the rain to meet the seed.

Into a crater she the "Bird of Paradise" is tossed,
A tribute that, if efficacious, means eruption lost

And lava halted. To alleviate a market crash
There is no ritual. We might, of course, torch into ash

A Joan of Arc of Wall Street, Hetty Green–like in her zeal,
Or turn her—Ixiona?—on a giant Keno wheel;

Betroth her, as a Phantom of the Opera pipe organ
Peals, to a paupered double, nose and all, of J. P. Morgan.

Most of sacrifice is ego, surely. In the end
It vaunts one god and that one limelight. Unto him ascend

Descents of virgins in addition to the smoke of Joan.
The job description of a martyr rules out little known.

Depend on envy, too, to put such where they are. A faith
Itself, it uses as its Wrath of God plain garden wrath.

The plunging maidens, plunging markets, lift the two gods praise
And chart their futures: Corn, the good-year, lean-year brief of days;

Eternal Fire, for all its blue and orange ups and downs
Utility like any other, off when Pele frowns.

The vortex deepens; rivals plot; the roaring mountain towers.
Such are the enemies of youth. Mere gravity is ours.

Vegetarian Mary and the Venus Flytrap

It is not edible, but if one ate it . . .
For the paradox it poses should one hate it?
Where upon the food chain to locate it?

Would a salad of it or a souffle
(Soufflé lacking egg white) be at one removal
Eating meat, and have the disapproval

Of the dietarily correct?
Would Fundamentalist teetotalers be wrecked
If Pitcher Plants should drown their prey in *Sekt*?

(Insekticide: destroying bugs in bubbly.)
To think of eating meat unknowing troubles doubly.
I shall sew my lips up and starve glubly

(Glumly; I am writing with a cold)
One-upping native Ecuadorians of old,
Who only sewed the lips of others, sold

To ethnocentricists as shrunken heads.
Not all species are those protected by the Feds.
The franchise is a Panama Club Med's.

Med-Sea-Born Goddess into insect trapping,
Permit that as a grain of irritation, capping
My career of vegetary flapping,

I seed your natal shell: the inner, all
Encompassing correctness—amnesty-in-general—
Where, pure pearl, I end as mineral.

James Jones, Infantry

1921-1977

I was no massive intellect; still, I was not a fool.
I was, as that decade I hated would have put it, "cool."

Belated and displaced, was I, in an exotic tryst,
Backhandedly, the 1930s' greatest novelist?

Hawaii is forever what I made it: Schofield, Pearl,
Hotel Street . . . uniforms and uniforms, the beach, B-girl,

And preying tourist. By comparison with my roll call
The Steinbeck Joads seem alienated really not at all.

Count Tolstoy was, in any last analysis, a count;
Blind Homer blind especially to those who ride no mount.

I brought to page the good sense of the unremarkable.
I put in print the mind of those who have no mind but will.

Count Leo; John; pretentious, foolish Norman; poet Rud;
Here is my body; here is, page on honest page, my blood.

Lift up a bugle, you, to art, to me, and to the hurt
Arms heal. To some eternal dogface in a floral shirt.

Repenting the Needle, Somewhat

So many sins one has to live with;
So little patience to forgive with.

Was a single folly missed?
As if proceeding down a list

One checked off all: extravagance,
Self-centeredness, escape, romance.

The use of pain for pure display;
Bravura, shallowness. Or say

These: Sacred Heart, God, Mother, Flag,
Knife, serpent, eagle, " Bash a fag."

Embarrassing also, blood type,
Serial number, unit, stripe.

Would one have missed them if one could?
Tattoos on young skin may look good.

Deep Depression in Key West

In vehicles that travel only south,
We camp from isle to isle and hand to mouth.

You South downhill from Ozarks and from Smokies,
Cockroach Country, greet us Counter-Okies.

California ceases at the pier;
The sea itself drops off six miles from here.

One town with just two things to do. No more.
Become a sailor or become a whore.

My wife gets seasick; I'm not very cute.
The tourists fish a lot; we'll follow suit.

The coffee's Cuban and the pie Key Lime.
Right now it's "Sailor, can you spare a dime?"

Days of Labor

As if the Chinese Wall in its repute
As cemetery had become a source
Of envy, hurricane allows the West
The Overseas Highway. And, life for life,
Who is to say the Highway's cost per mile
Does not exceed the Wall's, or that, in its
Evasive New Deal way, the C.C.C.
Was not forced labor? Coolies of the Keys,
Backwater conscripts, those who here were drowned
No more rise up to haunt a tourist trade
Than years of the Imperial corvée
Come back in kind to haunt the Communists.
If they are not themselves memorials,
The Thiepval Arch, the Vietnam Wailing Wall,
Construction projects do not name the names
Or tell the tales.
               Key Largo in September,
1935. A rescue train
Backs out toward Marathon, it being that
The engine crew insists upon. If wind
Derails the coaches they can be cut loose
And let the locomotive go for broke.
The barracks and the tent encampments—bridge,
Key, bridge—are rope that flies and roof that flaps.
It is a trial of survival skills
For those who have not shown them. Engine first,
A full week later, when the tracks are cleared,
A train of flatcars picks the bodies up:
A Buchenwald of nature, though the Corps
Has sense enough to burn the photographs.
And in the mangrove swamps the fishing boats
Discover Southern trees bear *quite* strange fruit.

Necks broken in the forking of the limbs,
Or spines along the sand like railroad ties,
As bondsmen over whom the wheels roll past,
As " hornless goats" of voodoo sacrifice
(And efficacious; Highway One exists)
To Cracker labor comes success at last.
Tour Group, if you would see their monument . . .

Dante by the Bay

A shifting silver at the edge of sight—
Horizon, but not quite—
The offshore fog stands-off the night:

Uncertainty diffusing, as it nears,
The all too certain. Piers
Reach out, in inshore haze that clears,

Safe harbor from a two-part darkness cleft
As all the silvers lift
And true horizon is what's left.

The wisdom of convention is, the black
On top is sky, the lack
Of light below is sea. To take

On faith is to accede to limits. Have
Instead the air above
Be where the primal life forms strove,

And underneath where, slaves of duty, sun
And other stars, as one,
Believe they move for love, or none . . .

And see all night reduce to the absurd:
No sphere or music heard,
No Earth in which we are interred.

Red Rust in the Sunset

The lagging wave hangs whitely just behind the bow,
And in the calm that it divides a tramp slips out.
Outlasting yachts and liners—it may be, their Lines—
Ad hoc by definition, chance's charter, luck's
Vague cruise outside the twelve mile limit, tramping pays,
Its truest capital its mockery of plan,
Its Brass cut to a strictest pattern: devious.
The Culture of the Bridge is everywhere the same:
Odysseus on board would know just where he was;
Could take the tiller, turn a profit, turn a phrase.
And could Magellan? Circumnavigators' dreams
Are no Greek eye toward the main chance, Portuguese as speech
Or flag convenience. A vessel well designed
Entails no wake to speak of, nor an art excess:
Only a thin bow-wave to quill the cutting edge;
An unintended cargo dealt with as it comes;
Distinct from an itinerary, a careful course
Among close isles of dalliance, where vengeance waits;
The keeping of the watch, that will at last keep you;
A lined-off log that is your life; the life that log;
Its unknown payout in the last long port of call.

From *Watchboy,*
What of the Night?

1966

Haitian Endymion

What partial dark, inverting on the sea
A melon with a rind of indigo,

What shadow in that riper night beyond,
Will hide the final dark I face from birth,

Who in the create darkness now my skin
See uncreated nothingness to come,

And in the tomb of the mosquito net
Seek out a sleep that dreams itself enough;

Who sleep, and am the nude somnambulist
For whom the flesh becomes sufficient cause,

When, risen in a sky no longer night,
La Belle Diane sinks toward the dark she leaves,

And of my body, naught that will not die,
Conceives the crescent margin that is life.

Aubade

Spacing with dark the light that we evade,
The single shutter stripes the sun with shade.

A striate flesh upon a striate sheet,
You are your hair, eyes, mouth . . . and thus to feet.

Two staggered bodies, one these bands of light,
The other, parallel confines of night,

You are in one self cosmos paced with sleep,
Chaos in whom fragmented rhythms keep.

And though one dream of order, when he mates
He is a chaos that perpetuates.

Momently, on these squares of swept rattan,
Our lizard voyeur, wearying of man,

Debates if he will circle, or will not,
The microcosm of the chamber pot.

And for the little time that he delays,
And in their far-out, citronella daze

His small familiars the mosquitoes dart
But do not strike—lie near me but apart.

As fever and as carrier, as force,
As loss, love soon enough will run its course,

Through sweat, through cramp, to be in its last breath
Receptacle, evacuation, death.

Teatro Amazonas

(Manaus)

Mosaic sidewalks phase the downcast vision,
And where it lifts, the solid dome has pulse—
As if that after-image, wholly motion,
Unfettered structure from the space it fills;

As if the silent house, its lush imprudence,
Were image only: focus, in pure void,
Of such bent rays as cultures in decadence
Fan outward to excite the dark they dread.

Extreme response bright in the heart of darkness,
Its awkward, beaux-arts force unworn by years,
The ornate folly conjures, all uniqueness,
Its belle époque of rubber millionaires.

Is it illusion that, to caned seat bottoms,
A sweating Bernhardt droned the chill Racine?
Illusion too, that ferried here as totems,
European singers, un-divine,

Unvaccinated, died of yellow fever?
Or have mirage and structure one live base:
Mute caryatids on whom rest forever
Art, folly, wealth, and the clear insights of ease;

Who, bearing still each headstone of their burden,
Solicit drop by drop the sticky trees;
Who know, how when the saps of nature harden,
Whips seek in time another in its place;

And who cannot know, how, for those who wield them,
It is enough that on brute darkness, rows,

One color, specify which forces yield them;
Until the spectrum and the blood oppose,

And dim all color downward. Red . . . magenta . . .
Full darkness: when the builders struggle home,
And what was exclave ends as irredenta;
When caryatids rise and heave the dome.

A Message from Mother Goddam

Scattered our smoke, uprooted now the poppy:
What dream, Taipan, did your delusion copy,

That as in a dream the yellow millions
Should on these mud flats raise you stone pavilions?

Until that city, still not real, seem wholly
Their pleasure dome to ease your melancholy,

And on the Bund, in solace of your boredom,
The jerking rickshas pull their weight of whoredom.

What vision seeks here to preserve forever
Each gleam, each mist of this imagined river?

Mirage or water, there, at humid dawnings,
The idle gunboats let out canvas awnings;

Marshaled at evening in the White cantonments
Your putteed garrisons ward old alignments.

It is yourself they guard. When, dream unshaken,
You sleep on, and the dreamless sleepers waken;

When, riven with a dream's withdrawing thunder,
The treaties crumble and the ports go under,

Where then is your identity—whose vesture,
Substance, essence, all vanish in a gesture;

Whose future, retrospective and uncertain,
Is this illusion through a beaded curtain.

La Petite Tonkinoise

I am not person, and am not opinioned.
I exist as I have been companioned.

You create me. Legionnaire or Viet,
I was your Somewhere East of Cigarette;

As I shall be, for grown-up Terry, beady
Eyed as ever, real-life Dragon Lady—

Anna May Wong, or, Soong once more, and young,
A not so avaricious Madam Chiang.

All pirate, you, the lanky, latest comer,
Jump-booted, trample the eternal summer;

Pausing only when, like any drab,
I cycle past you on a pedicab.

As the tight skirt scissors, so the ankle hinges.
While it does, no other change impinges.

Yet I and wheel, meek where your glance is hurled,
Combined, were Fortune, Empress of the World.

Were each reversal. I that stony bosom,
Parachute and you the broken blossom;

Who, even now, hear in the anklets' ring
No warning—only jada, jada, jing

Jing jing.

Calvin in the Casino

(He apostrophizes a roulette ball)

Sphere of pure chance, free agent of no cause,
Your progress is a motion without laws.

Let every casuist henceforth rejoice
To cite your amoralities of choice,

By whose autonomy one apprehends
The limits where predestination ends;

Where the Eternal Will divides its See
In latitudes of probability,

And the divine election is obscured
Through being momently and long endured.

It is obscured and is rejustified,
That stands fulfilled in being here denied,

Lest its caprice should lead the mind to curse
Some biased and encircling universe,

Or its vagaries urge us to reject
That one same Will which chooses the elect.

Woman

(From the Afrikaans of Elisabeth Eybers)

The lesser seasons pass in wide,
Sure exodus across a land
Where she retains the Spring, whom love
Exalts one season out of time.

Hate and destruction fix elsewhere
The standards of the night. In her,
Whom blood, whom struggle also wait,
Peace and well-being echo still.

The horseman halts, the sickle lowers;
And in the distance of her glance
Death measures his dominion's end.

She summons, ward of timelessness,
All futures in the faint reflex
Of life forever re-begun.

Watchboy, What of the Night?

Do you envision, in this night
Which is your being and your end,
The outworn night you half renounce,

Or do you, where your sidewalk fire
Is hearth and future, guard the light
So lately come, so hardly kept,

Signaling now from every street
The one response: unchange, content;
As if the omen were itself

Its own denial, and the man
Who watches in the night were all—
Protector, danger, oracle.

Servant Problem

(Johannesburg)

High wind across the mine dumps, and in shining air
The shining grit. In winter sunlight, lemon-clear,
A million small reflectors settle on the stair.

Indifference in his mind and push broom in his hand,
The flat-boy, function less than ornament, unmanned
In being always boy, malingers: bits of Rand,

Ignored, remain. Shall I submit or shall I scold?
The ornament is lame and sixty-five years old.
The not especially unsettled dust is gold.

A Somewhat Static Barcarolle
(Amsterdam)

Neutral and dull, the bricks that serve as shores
Enforce their color on the channeled water;
And if a distant movement, as of oars,
Has made that mirrored brick, its mortar scatter,
Now, as the soon abated force goes slack,
A leveling inertia lays them back.

Surface on surface to a depth of peace—
How little stirred to be so far from stagnant!
As if reflection and its slow release,
Its visions idly on that water regnant,
Themselves were substance and renewal; beat
Or silence; action, and the act complete.

As if our shadows, lengthening below,
Received us bodily to calm, to vision,
Always to rock with lifted oars; where, low
Beside the mirror, sense and its precision
Give to the arching sky, the dormered town,
A motion one brick up and one brick down.

Junker-Lied

(Schleswig-Holstein)

More than myself (estate, degree),
I discipline my world to me,

For whom the viewpoint fills the view;
For whom all things become these few:

Four pinnacles and four clear ponds,
A quartered sky that corresponds;

The charted cattle, maps of peace,
And white ellipses which are geese.

If, in the dream's contempt of truth,
A goosegirl first is swan, then youth . . .

Awakened, would he see in mine
Seducer's eyes and base design,

Or only see what he may know,
That evil's grace is not to show.

Could he distinguish, did he try,
Which is the eyeglass, which the eye.

Love in Cincinnati

In comfort, soot and snow lose each their rigors.
Our backdrop fits *Bohème*, but we are burghers;

And through our windows, in that moving stipple,
Go past the figures of the not quite people:

Intermittent, partial, pointillistic—
No more a likeness than if we, bold, plastic,

Entire, unmade them by our mere example;
Than if our bodies (counting house, not temple)

Housed yet a spirit they, for all their motion,
Cannot warm. Who treasures inhibition,

Here, may find it, in its late expressions,
Unearned income that supports the passions;

Find also, laying-by whatever wounded,
How middle age returns it all compounded.

Accruing time, of what unlikely mortar,
Has built us thus a burgess Latin Quarter:

Of red brick rectitude and iron repression
Improvised this gaslit indiscretion,

And placed about us, linked to love's warm center,
The populated streets we now must enter.

Period Piece

Leather helmet, lifted goggles,
Out of the cockpit Lindbergh struggles—

Henceforth, accident or plan,
Anything but Everyman:

Icarus intact, all Paris
His, and, his to be, an heiress;

While the honest press chants still
"Ambition, self-reliance, will."

Yet, goggles lowered, helmet fastened,
Photographed, he so is chastened;

Grown a skull, thus put upon,
He must himself cry Jedermann;

As though foreseeing loss, the Axis,
Graduated income taxes;

Seeing corporate, bland thoughts
Which are the minds of astronauts,

And how one hears an honest press
Chant "Teamwork, peace, togetherness."

Grace at the Atlanta Fox

Whenever, in that ceiling sky,
Familiar clouds once more go by,

And in the restrooms, far below,
One half the lamps of Islam glow;

When, overweight but overawed,
Undying Grace, Eternal Maude

Once more are en rapport—are one—
With Myrna Loy and Irene Dunne

(Irene as essence, Maude; Ur-Myrna:
Now the new star Annapurna,

Nepalese and thick of tongue);
Or when, pure movie, pure, brave, young,

The Foreign Legion dare and do,
Each year is 1932;

Pre-Eleanor, pre-war, pre-Fala;
Time as place: the Garden of Allah,

Near whose entrance, chill with freon,
That time's great sign resists still neon,

To be through Moorish, Hoover nights
This fugue of incandescent lights;

As if to make some statement yet;
As if the tan brick minaret

Were point and counterpoint; not theme,
But theme to be, that when the dream

Maude dreams is ours, and we too nod,
States then "There is no God but God . . ."

Of Heaven as Production Number

Perspective false and canvas full of tears,
The painted backdrop terminates real stairs;

And toward that point at which they vanish, paint
Or hole, an act of faith impels, not saint

But mediocrity. Sure his trite steps
Somewhere will be writ large, a dancer taps

Intent as though some new dimension yawned.
It yawns. There on the screen, on its surround,

A black and white aurora throws with ease
A staircase of immense piano keys;

Ascending which, in top hats, nothing more,
Pure-tonic chorus girls tap out the score.

Angelic Evas in angelic curls;
Angelic Topsies in melanic pearls,

And in the center, dancing as he did,
The unimproved and undone hominid:

Machine-writ large upon the starry void,
Yet flattened thereby into celluloid;

Who, in the round, by slowly failing strength,
Learned there is only width and breadth and length,

To be dispelled one stairstep at a time,
However often still he may, in time,

Have dreamed of escalation and an end—
An easy rise through Credits to The End,

And there, a heaped-up female ziggurat
As perfect summit to transfigure at.

A Song in Subtitles

The timeless shadow, infinite of reach,
Declines in time from silence into speech.

You, idol of our finite time and place,
Who spoke me, accent wholly without grace,

My common need and its specific steps,
Repeat them still, but only move your lips;

And all your motions, gauche or overtrained,
I have remembered. I have freed, restrained.

Such eloquence as they have now is mine.
It is the art these actors, grown pure line,

Attain through being mute; and their myth, you,
So much more pre-existent now, seem too;

Until the simple gesture (more is less)
Brings back the other side of consciousness;

And they and we, in silence beyond sound,
Re-enter what is there, or is not found.

A Song to Be Syndicated

Not nearly there, our rebirth journey wrecks.
We are the Katzenjammer Kids with sex;

And must again, in early adolescence,
Act out the dual and destructive presence.

I am Hans, dark still, still true to type.
In short, I am a shadow archetype.

You, recognizable behind your tan,
Are still incipient blond superman,

Too alien for twin, too close for brother.
But here is Mama, otherwise Great Mother,

And here the Captain—all that burgherdom
We take up arms against, and would become.

Inspector, bored *voyeur* of what old crime,
Seem rather, by your bearded visage, Time.

Break, Time, these frames and set us free: cured freaks
Borne oppositely down the strip of weeks;

I, in the flat balloons my set speech fits,
Always to say, "Auf Wiedersehen, Fritz."

Domestic Symphony

I sell securities, and am artistic.
Your career is somewhat more elastic.

Not quite viable but not quite kept,
Which would you be if you were less inept?

I pay and cope, deny you, house, indulge.
You keep in training: swagger, ripple, bulge.

Here, in this décor layer after layer
High to middle Metro-Goldwyn-Mayer,

You are Tarzan, I am Baby Jane.
If, earlier, we each were Boy, the gain

Is both a self and other. How it came
We know already. Mother was to blame.

Blame, then, and settle down to being other:
Tell me—I'm all self—you like me rather.

Tell me that, however strained its uses,
So late a compromise at least amuses.

Tell me use will ease that act of pride
Where each is cross and each is crucified.

Say Heaven is this tree house we have sinned in.
Our wine is ready. Pour, while I fix din-din.

A Clock with a Mirror Face,
Presented to a Lady

Because the hemispheres of day and night
Succeed each other faster than they might,
And in that interchange of night and day
The lumens of thy beauty wear away,
I give thee, measure of a smoother change,
A little world the dark cannot derange;
That substitutes, for circling of the sun,
Slow wheels that turn all moments into one;
That marks the interdicts, the pomps of time,
With noncommittal click and neutral chime,
Till change, diffused through uniform degrees,
Diminishes in wastes of litotes.

Turn therefore, with thy fragile beauty fast,
From transiences where beauty cannot last;
From where a chronometric universe
Clocks beauty's passing and is beauty's hearse.
Turn from the frictions of the flesh and bone
And contemplate denatured change alone.
Look only in this numbered mirror face
And find a timepiece that cannot erase,
Where fixed an instant beauty's image stands
Passed over carelessly by time's two hands.

Ways of Feeling

Here is the opened heart, and here the Calais:
    You the letters, you the loss.
The fresh incision you, the drug, the knife.
Mine is the threatened and surrounding life.

Too radical for more than partial cure,
    The not unwelcome message, late
Revealed, at last informs. Not much a lesson
Then, you teach me now my own discretion.

Who shows the sores becomes in time the leper.
    Who, his privacy his skill,
Has learned their language, knows, if surgeons fail,
An inexhaustible and cautious braille.

*From Scenes from
Alexander Raymond,
or,
The Return of
Ming the Merciless*

1971

I

His Supreme Intelligence,
the Emperor of the Universe

From the alien planet—prompt—the perfect hero;
He is heart, the action principle, hope, threat.
I am the Merciless. Above a high, stiff ruff,
An oriental distance in my eyes, a neck
Yellow and old. You know me. I am Klingsor here,
The Manchu doctor there: Dagon, as I was Baal.
Into my hands the infants offered, in my voice
Seduction that will gain for me the sacred lance.
Know, Earthling, if I set for you the chill ordeal,
It is that passion is the foe of polity,
And I am Emperor. My servile kings, who, flaws
In that perfection of my unity, foresee
And use you, use to foil. To their respective lusts
They will betray you in the end. I, only, spare;
Am worthy equal of your trust and of your hate.
The classic light, unbroken in so great remove,
Now breaks; it is the jagged current in your hair,
As it will be a cataract upon your helmet.
Achilles of the cleated heel, you will be seen,
If not preserved from harm. Move, therefore, in your blaze
Which fragments in event the purity of cause.
Seize! Dazzle! Act! Fame is to thrill eternity
By the sequential. Threaten me, that I should say:
After me will come one who is greater than I.
Yet know, I am eternal; that I shall not alter,
Yield, or pity. Though I spare you, I devise
In my own time my own revenge. I am yourself;
Am every art you have, and the deep space you probe,
The end, the source, the unmoved mover you must move.
Be greeted. From this core, unto the farthest stars,
My universe encloses on itself and glistens;
It the incandescent fruit and I the seed:
Center of centers, nucleus of nuclei.

II
Assorted Beasts

The tree limb calcifies, and in the colored cave
We go down toward the lighted water: living arch
Above the limestone. Hydra by the flat chalk pool,
We are one beast and we are many; veined as opal,
Uniform as emerald. Shine, twisted hide!
The dim, volcanic steam will heat us into life
And we shall take our old heraldic forms. Each horn,
Each leather wing, all shapes of eye, cry Nineveh.
The cavern echoes, and among the aisles of crystal
Comes a hale, Teutonic warrior; in his step
An earth that gives and in his gaze the sky that rains;
Wherefore we hate him. Torrent of the gleaming shaft,
Strong lower windstorm, fail him. While the giant cape
Streams outward like the nimbus of a great protection,
While the horsehair plume speaks on the skull in tongues,
We tremble. Shadow, pure chameleon, abstraction,
We are each defeated by the actual.
If, in that Garden without compromise, one fruit
Had of itself been cynosure sufficiently,
Guile were not now a serpent, knowledge not a bait.
The motif sounds; the choice is made. The sword is moving.
It is bared. The visual assaults us. Link,
Divided flesh. Become idea of idea.
Meet the act and meet the choice. Be indolence,
Be speculation; promise of the yet to choose.
Turn into willing fellator of your own tail—
Surrounded form, an ultimate Plato. The light!
The shining blade has sickled-through our perfect poise.
The ring destructs! We shatter into theory.
In dialogue, in trivialities of notion
Dissipates the vain, the parasitic blood.
Du helläugiger Knabe, unkund deine Selbst.
You slay by vision. Do you know whom you have slain?

III
A City in the Sky

Below us, thunderheads drift idly off their bases,
Parting where the slow wings pass them. Still we rise.
The still haze thins, as if to pass to stratosphere,
And we confront as flesh the dream metropolis;
Late, wingless captives to a city not of time.
As technocrats, we can, if not escape, explain.
Force-rays and forces of the racial memory pier it up:
The anything but sexless angels give it weight.
A Heaven of the literal, of hydroponic
Life the hanging garden; where the circling stairs
Are spirals unsupported, and the core skyscrapers
Downward daggers out of space. Resist them. We—
Demented, learned doctor; tall track star; undressed
And archetypal Follies beauty—now receive,
By turn, one same indenture. I and he to chains,
She to the sleek and long seraglios in the sky.
A little time to love, and afterward the steel.
The terms extend, and at the endless furnaces
Whose energies support the world, revolt is fired.
The shovels of our bondage, charged, ignite the ores.
Do not think, incorporeal state, now their force
Has failed you, eminence will save. The city tilts;
The rays that base it fail. Its clustered towers topple;
On the great staircases die the guard who lined them.
Transparent in the safety of their height, thrown wide,
Its glass and onyx harems plummet toward the pavement:
Lifelong purdah turned at last upon the streets.
I, who am mad, might save. Of thinnest air alone
Erect a city naught but balance: gyroscope
Of Heaven, undepending orchid fed on sun.
In disembodied love its law evaporates,
Ecology its only code. Its streets are free,
Its races one. Its enemies we melt for soap.

IV
Tournament

Heat rising and the sand new-raked. In waving air
Still banners ripple. By the barrier, enlarging
Tier to tier, one last concentric silence: mob
As vortex, amphitheater a waiting cymbal.
In the eye, the quiet center, we, too tense
To be professionals, too scarred for amateurs,
See through that shimmer trumpeters lift up their bells.
Turn from us, golden throat. You narrow toward the dark.
In narrowed breath the summoning abyss will speak;
Evoke us what has gone before, what yet will come:
How, on the long tightrope, the barren sky above,
Brimstone below, we dueled Abel to a draw,
To step on earth among his daggers set for path.
Arrayed in theory, he faces us again.
His sword is flaming. He has chosen that good part.
Who tells himself mute sky accepts his sacrifice
Returns to sacrifice us to it. Cain, meanwhile,
Accommodates the armor to the mark. His heralds
Draw their lips. At that first note, we who are he
Take up the red inheritance of spectacle;
Knowing that, in some continuing arena,
Tigers pace always, whose target, and whose cage,
Is confine of our own few ribs. If, in the tiers,
There are a thousand beasts, each wagers only once,
Each sides with us against the safety and the sheep.
The trumpeters attack: the twisting heat swirls up.
A tall whirlwind, dividing into four, lifts now
Above the taut profile a canopy of dust.
Hail, Majesty! We too have had our baldachin.
From this stark sun, the total scrutiny of zenith,
Unto other suns beyond, the universe
Here shrivels to the stained old round of sand. The lance
Goes upward on the note. *Morituri te salutamus.*

V
In the Palace of Blue Magic

Not much a lover. In the azure tapestries,
The bluestone, mediaeval rooms, already—drugged
Well out of self—he visibly is bored. The potion
Acts, the man accomplishes. One, all the same,
Is not much flattered. Hold the flagon in contempt,
My rudely subjugated love; it is the shade,
The obverse side of the domestic. You, so stiff,
So gauche, so wholly blunt, remember in your sleep
Each adolescent's dream of passion as a distance:
Object into object and the clean withdrawal.
There are women, they are many, who devise
Of any silence that late speech of their desire.
I am not one. I have my own postscripts of silence.
I shall hear you say no more than what you say.
The young read into: they are cheated. I read merely,
And am not deceived. Of all whom you have met,
I only have escaped the curse of pure ideal.
Sleep, then, and if you wake to bondage or to cure,
To lust or into impotence, the brute event
Need not concern you, since anecdote falls heir to all.
Speak of me, if you speak, as one so little patient
She obtained by sorcery to cast aside;
As mortal women, in their blind slow Platonism,
Cast aside to recreate. Dawn, inert flesh,
Is in this cave a phosphorescence on the stones.
It is sufficient, nonetheless, to cry for alba,
Nor is any love so strong it may refuse.
The sand-glass trickles and the white stalactite lengthens;
At his pace somewhere between the lone guard passes.
Blue the palace walls, and blue his shadow on them.
Farther, in the chasms where the light-stones wake,
Set free of time and sun, the beast of ideal day
Is systemizing. Sleep, Chaos, and I shall watch.

VI
The View from the Water World

Sun sparkling where the deeps lie open; duller jade
Deep in the canyons, in the calm. And shall the shells,
No more informers, in their chambers keep their peace?
Or, circumlocution yet their dialect, still warn;
Foretelling, "Dead or diver, be the motive greed
Or be it birth, let go the lamp; it is too late.
Ye cannot enter now." And all the years of salt
Upon the eyeball sting their confirmation. Blink!
Divide, Exile, your little waters from the great,
And be re-born. Upon the eye's wet underside
Conceive the sea as if you dwelled forever in it;
Moving in its motion, native to its speech.
Re-learn the pace that differs. Action, undersea,
Slows into ritual; to be detailed, examined;
Never losing, frame by frame, its sure legato.
Not the stroboscope itself can break that grace,
Fragment its smallest creatures' small continuum.
Who, awkwardly in time, assumes eternal form
Must, to the instants of his own rough crawl, stay blind.
The eye resists; the living swimmer comes to shore.
It is the hearer who will now address the shell.
I am no athlete of a marble wall. I sweat
Or shiver; know the tendons severed; feel my age.
Yet I am not so dull a body, some cartoon
So wholly as I have not too my dim ideal.
It may be obvious enough; it has, like most,
Its freight of vanity. Yet, balancing discreetly,
Not of sea, not land, it outwits element.
It is the vision of the diver. Is he I?
Through all the frozen moments I have been, I am:
One skill renewed among the springboard, self, and sea;
Amphibian denied; too vital for sheer stasis,
Too enduring to seem motion. Marble, yield.

VII
The Merciless Returns

Event transfigured and the sequence all but done,
We meet again, as I foretold. Heavier now,
The vain swan-diver in the years just after prime,
You listen with the inclined head, the faint new squint
That may mean interest, unease, or deafness. I,
Unchanged in any least respect, am, nonetheless,
A little differently perceived. The gold iguana,
Zodiac of the rapacious, still is crown;
Along the scepter still repose my almond nails.
It is not protocol that I should white my beard,
Or turn this scepter into sickle. Your own change
Confirms my alias, reveals you my dominion.
In the still arena, in the utter cave
You were not quite outside it; in the ancient deep
It told your breath. In the perfection of the dive
It hesitated, and, resuming, was its grace.
The planets know it, and the orbits undisclosed:
The outer cold. There is not space I do not rule.
Thus, Rebel, it is left alone to pass the sentence.
I am not without set pities. Who resist me,
It is they who name me Merciless. Who yield,
I hasten toward their fit reward. Fall: break from air
And take defeat for comfort. Its sure victories,
Your sons, are you. If I reveal them otherwise,
You need not know it. Yours, the stubborn other choice,
Narcissus always makes. Though I am not blackmailed,
As you have been *frisson* I make you this concession:
After you, no other wanderer, no probe
Shall find on any planet any form of life.
The clockwork Vikings circle, and the robots walk,
And neither quickens. Only you have been their blood.
In your distinction, I have emptied space forever.
Du kühnes, herrliches Kind! Precursor, *lebewohl.*

From *Steeplejacks in Babel*

1973

What the Sirens Sang

Who seals the ear sets free the eye.
No light we cannot enter by.

Green on the starboard, red to port,
The sea's directions pay you court.

They are the poles of your content;
And where you go and where you went

Divide you, who will not regain,
Unmarked, the certain course. One chain

Will rankle always on your wrist,
Along your spine be scored the mast.

Though, while you watch, the emerald
Phosphors and is a plural world,

Your former, deep and garnet, edges
Primally the wake's long wedge.

Choose: simple hearth you knew before:
Dexterous brass on a verdant shore.

All vision passes, and the choice.
Thereafter, will the wax have voice?

Advise you, "Let the graphic fire
Draw on the wall your whole desire—"

Night free of envy, free of sight;
And in the mornings (shape, not light),

Your sinister, domestic fate:
Home's still warm ash that fits the grate.

The Procurator Is Aware That Palms Sweat

The hands I wash, I wash advisedly.
The thief I pardon—he is freed to steal,
Theft being, by its nature, rendered thee,
And so the lesser evil. Caesar, Hail!

The vain young man who scourges, who is kissed,
Betrayed, himself is scourged, and all for youth,
May find, in dampened silver, truth I lost
In salvered water. Yes; but what is truth?

A Crown for the Kingfish
(The Huey P. Long Bridge, New Orleans)

Patrol car sirens, anywhere they're bound,
Are, finally, the sine curve done in sound.

In the vicinity of this one bridge,
Though formulary, they are still cortege;

As, underneath that publicizing steel,
The river is an earth and burial:

A redneck mud that past the creole streets
Parades its plethora of old defeats.

The pomps are their reciprocal. Each guard,
Each Buick, each machine-gun late reward

The early want. Innate, it nonetheless
Is colored, channeled, by its time and place.

No empire that the hearth has not rehearsed;
No leader who was not gauleiter first.

Utilitarian, yet arrogant,
A bridge is too exact a monument.

Its profile is the bow cut down and strung.
It is the weapon chosen, challenge flung;

Is hickory turned into metal: all
The taut boy was, and now, all he will be.

Cain precedes Adam, and the central tree,
If knowledge later, first is arsenal.

Manchuria 1931

Guard duty by the railhead, where the rails
Run into sand, and burlap on high bales

Is ragged in the wind. His angles steep,
The pack-train camel sleeps a shaggy sleep.

He sleeps; I yawn. I settle in my coat;
I feel the dry cold tighten in my throat.

I go on; east or west, I do not know.
Direction, absent in these sands below,

Above is blazoned in the clustered stars,
That chart us, light by light, their blue bazaars,

Their shining trade, their far-flung conquest. Dim,
Descending to the eastern, western rim,

They light, a little, parting caravans
That are their own horizon; or, intense

Among our errant locomotive sparks,
Align the several and smoking darks;

Until—an east of easts and type of types—
The rising sun stands in a sky of stripes;

And I can see, who feel it in my eyes,
A yellow sand that levels out the ties.

The Last of Vichy

(Dakar)

Dust on the harbor; high chutes coal the tramp.
The concrete villas darken in the damp,
And in the land they point to, I was born.
Alien color, be now alien corn.

One knows one's harvest. Can its site deceive?
Or will the soot, the stalagmitic, leave
Intact the live defeat, the treadmill flight,
The attitudinized pursuit. By right

My lot should be division. I am whole,
And have the whole. The parody is all.
Mansard and mosque, and tree-lined boulevards
So far from France, so near the livestock yards.

Long out of uniform, and going gray,
The Legion take the Tonkinese cafe.
They, irreducibly imperial,
German or blackface, always know their role.

I too have at my distance served my evil.
By it you endured. When you cavil
Bear in mind that in my brief high noon
I might have made this *Grösser Kamerun*.

Sandblasted into grandeur, pure, rebuilt,
Home may assume the profit, enjoy the guilt.
In each, there is assured support from Bonn.
I, meanwhile, live as though my side had won.

I note the headland through the brilliant haze;
Coffee and cocoa black and tan my days.
In the harbor that sustains one—vision, fortress,
Farce—one flies the colors of the port.

Pacelli and the Ethiop

The Italian government's representations to the Vatican's secretary of state, Cardinal Eugenio Pacelli, had their effect. The Holy See did not further condemn the potential aggressor.

—George W. Baer, *The Coming of the Italian-Ethiopian War*

Unlikely angels, although by and large well met,
The pontiff and the emperor embattle yet—
Their paradise Geneva's giant Follies set.

One is a stately, beady-eyed old barracuda,
One some crypto-Coptic, bearded living Buddha.
The League of Nations hears again the Lion of Judah:

"True, I am a slaver. Now, as true confessor,
I demand the Church inculpate the aggressor."
Whereat the Earthly Vicar, ever the recessor,

Recedes into his role as papal secretary.
"That queen whom you succeeded . . . Matabele Hari . . .
The fat one . . . Did you give her poison, Ras Tafari?"

"What is truth?" inquires the League, and then dissolves.
The exiled emperor is forced to sell his slaves;
The pontiff washes in the silver bowl that saves.

The Entrance of Winifred into Valhalla

The Festspielhaus remained an object of considerable embarrass-
ment. By the terms of Siegfried Wagner's will it was the sole prop-
erty of his widow Winifred, whom a denazification court placed in
1947 in the group of major collaborators with the Nazi regime.
　　　　　　　　　　　—Geoffrey Skelton, *Wagner at Bayreuth*

As if to judge, the gods survey a darkened house.
The music that has made them real will let them see.

Mystic abyss or simple pit, the orchestra
Divides and distances. They will be accurate.

Being eternal, they observe in those who watch
All who have watched here ever. Whom they now elect

Will link and will epitomize. In one reprieve
Endure the kings and Cosima, Herr Hitler, she,

And the aloof G.I.'s. If these, unwittingly
Or well aware, make up tradition, hers alone

Is that tradition's grandeur; who, as trustees must,
Will yield or will defy, will use and cast aside;

Will make her peace with evil, take her toll of good;
And further, having once delivered up her trust,

Will live with her decisions. Not the pure blood-Wagner,
Nor the Liszt incursion, nor the sons to come

Outrank that force whose only name is guardian;
Toward whose intent defer at last her agents: Reich,

The godless shades of Weimar, and the gods themselves;
Who, merciless of eye and sensible of heel,

Not looking back, sets foot upon the Rainbow Bridge.

Blood and Flatiron

Stiff in the fitted uniform
Starch as idea: for the warm,

Wet skin the warning touch of chill;
In the indifferent fabric, will.

In the façade becoming slack
It is the cool, implied rebuke.

Starch is how vanity, how care,
Have made the shirt a shirt of hair,

And on the dripping, tropic site
Create the drillground anchorite—

Himself that shaft he occupies
And he as desert of its rise.

Chevrons or stigmata, the signs
Embellish only. Discipline

Is under, in the stubborn shape
That forms the cross or fights the nape;

That, neither line nor meaning, means
The more. Its message: how to seem.

It sketches, on the body's tense
Attention, rest without suspense.

The faint, defiant show of ease
It answers with a knife-edge crease:

There on the flesh its outlines smother,
The hard and vegetable other.

Carpenters

Forgiven, unforgiven, they who drive the nails
    Know what they do: they hammer.
  If they doubt, if their vocation fails,
    They only swell the number,

Large already, of the mutineers and thieves.
    With only chance and duty
  There to cloak them, they elect and nail.
    The vinegar will pity.

Judas who sops, their silver his accuser, errs
    To blame the unrewarded.
  They guard the branch he hangs from. Guilt occurs
    Where it can be afforded.

Purdah in Pretoria

The corrugated iron vibrates in thunder;
On the covered sidewalk, sun. Far under,
Gallon cans of bloom, and I the vendor.

Matronly, no lissome violet seller,
I ornament an air forever stiller:
I the turbulence and I the color.

Group unproven, area obscure,
Eviction certain. This is how I parry:
Caste mark, lipstick, corset, sari.

Blue, the jacarandas by my corner
Tangle in the lightning. On the burner,
Sidewalk curry draws the true discerner.

Old friends still are best. I once was svelte,
He the Vice Squad in a Sam Browne belt.
Hale and red and Dutch Reformer, well

Toward middle age, in shade already gusty
He precedes the hail.
                    The alley's dusty,
So I indicate my door. "Tea, Rusty?"

Confederates in Brazil
(1866)

Unreconstructed, uncontrite,
We seek the land that we have known by night.
The state of day we can endure to lose.
Never the dark of ancient use.

So long as, on the latticed vine,
The torrid moonlight seeps its gold and brine,
And in the garden pools the flashing carp
Give back its colors, but more sharp,

In that wet tension, haze on water,
Hang yet the motes cast out as of no matter:
Indulgence, common forms, observance, ease;
And, suspended even as these,

Their last illusion: continuity.
Sustain, night, still the same, still other,
Haze and past. By thy filled eye
Make one the mote and beam, the slave and brother.

DeLesseps Go Home

(Culebra, 1889)

The drunk Jamaicans cease to ditch, and I,
In fever, lay the unreal tripod by.

Surveyor, contract labor, we alike
Learn by delirium to yield the dike

That we are not the Dutch Boys of. Be brave,
And any stock exchange will dig your grave.

Far ticker tape and white liana, bell
Or sky of glass, what have you made us sell

That we should see, as if we fired them still,
Cold engines of the serpent's cloven hill?

Hospital, need I say, goes on. Brass bed,
Enamel bedpan, nun with leaden tread.

Have you in Picardy, *Ma Soeur, Ma Chère*,
A world whose savings are invested here?

Say to them: on the mole at Port Said
Their idol stands who fails us in our need;

Who, though he once built there on sand, displays
Here that clay will be his feet of clay:

That green and sugared hope burns off as dunder;
That it will not be we who put asunder.

Tripod and fever, Mother Combat Boots,
Qualify the prophet. By his fruits

You know him: by the dirt trains whose each car
Is painted U.S.A. or U.A.R.;

That seem this rust we see, but that will haul,
Piecemeal, the toppled idol off the mole.

New vine-shoots fill the firebox edge to edge;
Fresh-water fishes repossess the dredge.

Gauchesco

The dying cattle stumble from the mallet,
Who, however, stumbled toward it. He,
Their late conductor, spreads his shawl for pallet
To lie down by the chinaberry tree.

Fermenting berries move by on the blood;
Four chickens peck and swallow. Merry eyes
And bloody apron, blood upon his cards,
The old man deals a solitaire and plays.

The game comes out; the cows queue up and bellow.
Lighting charcoal in a punctured drum,
He waits. The waiting beef is thick with tallow;
The chickens have red bosoms and are drunk.

The Shropshire Lad in Limehouse

From Wapping Stairs to Limehouse Reach,
Warehouses rise six stories each;
And if their pilings, where I boat,
At low tide smell of creosote,

On the street side, they and their cables
Are London's Hanseatic gables;
And toward that sign of Aryan blood
I forge on through the tidal mud.

My manly form, my yellow hair,
My rower's torso partly bare,
Will bring to St. Anne's Limehouse steeple
Tonio Kröger's blue-eyed people.

From Pennyfields to Wapping High
I cross the road and pass on by.
The public school that tames the beast
Brings out the Levite, or the priest;

And though I am not of the breed
That leaves a man and lets him bleed,
The chink, the wog, the frog, the toad,
Have put themselves outside the code.

Still porting on my head my scull,
I met a dialectic trull.
And while I could not quite determine,
I rather think that she was German;

For, when the viaducts shut tight
Their early colonnade of night,

And later, when each light is red,
I quite remember what she said:

Denn die einen sind im Dunkeln,
Und die andern sind im Licht,
Und man siehet die im Lichte,
Die im Dunkeln sieht man nicht.

In Sydney by the Bridge

Cruise ships are, for the young, all that which varies.
The aged disembark with dysenteries.
Always, it is middle age that sees the ferries.

They hold no promise. Forward or reverse
Impels them only to where what occurs,
Occurs. Such is, at least, the chance of being terse,

And is their grace. The lengthy liners, fraught
Sublimely, shrill for tugs. If they're distraught,
That is because the thoughts of youth are long, long thoughts—

Save those of gratitude. The slow, massed force
That frees them they will cast off in due course,
To learn, or not to learn, the ferries' sole resource:

How, in the crowding narrows, when the current
Runs in opposition and the torrent
Claws the wheel, to locate in routine, abhorrent

For the storm, the shore that makes it specious;
Where one calls the vicious, curtly, vicious,
And the scheduled ferry, not the cruise ship, precious.

By the Waters of Lexington Avenue

> In place of a world there is a *city*, a *point*.
>
> —Oswald Spengler

Their rivet guns the noise of lily gilding,
Steeplejacks top out the Chrysler Building,
Which is height, and the idea height.
Tongue unconfused and the begun complete,

It will evoke us still that pride which beckons
And the sky it arrogates; that tokens,
On the equal plain, all enterprise
And all distinction. In its rise

Diminish sun-dried brick, harp, worker, river.
Held in that bright steel, there shine, forever,
Grounded lightning and the closing storm,
The ticker tape and the cuneiform.

Now, Exile, when the rivets cool in silence
And the hot sky waits, two forces balance:
Derrick, and the pinnacle it lifts.
The summit locks in place: the concrete shafts

Anticipate the elevator cables.
Neither harp nor pendulum, their able,
Twanging sound must yet pursue you; home
The exile, time the long captivity they strum.

But for that little while the shafts stay silent,
And at their climax, jerking, brilliant,
Lightning waits for thunder, will to power
Then conquers the quotidian. Pure tower

Stands. Let the reach and moment stand for all:
These tethered skies, and space through which they fall;
New conquests, age, the music it debars;
A Wall Street lunar skyline, Shinar, Mars.

L'aigle a deux jambes

(On a photograph of Sarah Bernhardt in L'Aiglon)

Eagle into swayback Ganymede,
The predator and prey become one breed;

Crippling Time the only Metternich,
Ego the only cup. As pallid duke,

For all the jack boots and the ducal sash,
You still are the devouring mother—ash

The taste, compulsive the desire. If Jove
Had finally his nectar, what you have

Is this: bankruptcy, fright wig, and a limp.
But while you've alexandrine for your pimp

You ravish; cruel in the knowledge that,
Olympian at last, you serve your fate;

Intransigence your courage, myth your art,
A rarer bird, a truer Bonaparte,

Across the steppes of your decay—in drag—
You stump toward Moscow on a wooden leg.

Off the Freeway

The all night station, vertical as noon,
To all that shades returns the shadow. Moon

And planet, other moons, above the pumps
The lettered globes shine on the garbage dumps,

To make of No-Knock and of New Lead-Free
Their Ptolemaic, fixed astronomy.

Born to the signs and system closed, the neo-
Magus trapped here would, if Galileo

Rose again to threaten now his franchise,
Cry "Lynch the Socialist" to save the ranch house.

It is not paid for, but one has for hope
The closing stock quotes, crosswords, horoscope.

One dozes, letting fall the loan shark's pencil.
Outside, wind chimes the advertising tinsel.

The vended foods are going brightly rotten;
Two empty pumps seem *Frauen ohne Schatten*.

In the dreams of enterprise still free
No bell for service sounds, no horns decree.

And what one does not see need never mock—
This past, this present, where one does not look:

The turning tinsel, brilliantly awake;
The young attendant, frankly on the make.

The Dispositions of Retirement Pay

Late naps, loose ends. The twenty year enlistment up,
The good life it prepared still tentative as sleep.

Gin, orange juice. The sunny condominium,
Paid fully, now is trophy, now the trophy room.

Jet lacquer out of Hong Kong, teak, authentic brass.
New Guinea and the Marshalls, Indo-China twice;

And if they loom always, or if they quite recede,
The form they gave continues: ease, but as the need

Demands, the small-scale talent given honestly.
Ease, what will the demand hereafter be? To say,

Of any idle love, it challenges? Or, once
The challenge has evaporated, to renounce

Each as a blackmail: one more trip-wire in the hurried,
Shallow side-world where the patently unmarried

Form a jungle on their own. Part of the time
A part time job will partly fill. If, wholly grim,

It will not call the whole man forth again, it may
In pity, dull the knowledge he is far away,

Still planning, in whatever jungle end is means.
All is as planned, yet somehow cheat. The razor hums;

The paper and the morning lie outside the door.
The inexperienced young man is forty-four.

Making Blackberry Jelly

In gallon cans, the berries fill the kitchen:
One of red to eight of ripe. Escutcheon,

Challenge of the wholly confident,
Her labels—dated, as if vintage meant—

Already mark the glasses. Never once
The aid of Sure-Jell, "never once one ounce

To turn to sugar." White, the cotton sacks
Await that purple they will strain. Attacks

(Appendicitis) come from eating seeds,
And jam does not quite suit the artist's needs:

The primal urge to seal in paraffin
Some essence wholly clarified. Thick, thin,

Remain the juices all which they have been.
The loose white blossom on the pale green vine;

These tiny chandeliers as dark as wine.
Clustering seed-pearls turned to red, the time

Of ripeness, and the other time of dread—
The liquid flood of birth, its jelling dead.

Pour out the total, for the rest is chance;
Pectin will shape now, or ferment advance.

Seal! Tyrian purple is from cotton wrung;
The whole of sense is gathered on the tongue.

Costuming the Pageant

The neat fire falters in the polished grate;
The treadle, oiled and mute, fails at such rate

As daylight and the ankle fail. Stout seamstress,
Is the robe you sew your one remonstrance—

Satin, tinsel—for this winter room
And year round solitude? Or in that tome

(The Doré Bible) open on your Singer
Is the pattern all: a wire coat-hanger

Bent for halo, cheesecloth cut for wings.
And if each host that with the angel sings

May also be, aloft in close formation,
Lucifer and cohorts, age and gumption

Are the lance to keep him still at bay.
Now, on her fingers—late—community

Has marked its own. Tenacious brass, the tinsel
Stains. Out of season, not the cup and chancel,

Yet communion all the same. She takes,
Receiver, giver of the gift she makes:

A gold, a frankincense of usefulness,
And myrrh of old achievement, strong to bless.

The practiced poker will command the embers;
Out of the treadle will the angel come.

Visiting the Cemetery

Who of these ordered dead, the named and grouped,
Has lost particularity? Descript,

If curtly, dated by the mason's art,
They form a whole of which she knows each part:

A branching genealogy in stone.
The stone tree flowers: the lineal, made one

In floral line with the collateral,
Have each the bloom her yard-man puts on all—

The eighteen small glass jars, as many flowers.
Upright, the yard-man stoops. His mistress towers.

Afternoon is quiet, and is not;
As if the dead were so much unforgot

They had a far, familiar pulse. Again,
Again, the sawmill sounds and is the kin.

If, when the Negro tends her grave as well
(It being somehow tacit that he will);

If her stone means to no one, least to him,
Well-being and the warm continuum,

Do these consanguine join the nondescript?
The lumber says deny, the shade accept.

Between, the dead are what they were. For what they are,
The early jonquil glistens in the mason jar.

Cartography Is an Inexact Science

The known world ends, and of the map's vague monsters
    We are one:
    A beast to fill in blanks.
    Not limits, but the limits passed,

We thrive a little, one the other's climate,
    Our two backs
    A sort of landfall. Drift,
    For all who come there, almost warms.

Behind us in those bordered lands, does custom,
    Growing old,
    Map still? Must all who love,
    In time, elaborate this unknown edge?

From *Yellow for Peril, Black for Beautiful*

1975

Allegory with Lay Figures

In dark blue suits intently go
The brisk young men of Tokyo.

They scorn the scooter, purchase cars,
They meet their girls in coffee bars.

The town they own is haze and tint.
They, nothing of a woodblock print.

Rather, intelligence, skill, drive—
High future that does not arrive.

Offset, non-rectilinear,
Their streets still grid them where they are.

Their city's fallout dusts the foot;
They wet their lips and taste a soot.

Malign old women vend them news;
The sea's own ancient shines their shoes.

Symbols (Shinto) line his scrapers.
Fake cherry blossoms drape the papers.

Dawn, the pure unable, whore
To all potential, banks.
                              Before,

Brush strokes in place and vowels stressed,
Electric signs fuse toward their rest.

The Press's witches close their arbor;
Drunk, the bootblack strolls the harbor.

The Love Life of Captain Hook

nur eine Waffe taugt

Wisely, the conformation—bright, curved, cruel—
Disdains to imitate the hand. If duel,

Be the duel not of flesh and copy
But of form and form. Iron though the grip he

Curbs, warm the hook he teaches, still their tension
Sparks our timely, obscene speculation:

Captain, does your sharp prosthesis love?
Fulfill, in its detachment, its remove,

The closest function? Or, stubbornly unbidden,
Fumble at the end the crucial button?

"This steel, Exile who mourn the land of Never,
Grows adept with use. Will you discover,

In a hand that stiffens when it ages,
Gesture I have learned by love's slow stages?

Curiosity, response, rebuff;
Or else a drawn blood that is love enough.

And if it comes of leather, strap, and screw,
Why then, your action is contrivance too.

You jerk the wire. True touch, true time, form after,
When the metal feel seems somehow softer,

And our futures, if not open book,
May be a sleight of hand and sleight of hook—

Their close few tricks our only Never. Reach!
The fingerless, the fingers, each to each,

Transmit the message our one wound deserves.
'Be whole, be healed. One weapon only serves.'"

Yellow for Peril, Black for Beautiful
(Honolulu)

The house is trim, the lawn chairs strewn with *Life*.
The Negro sergeant has a Chinese wife.

She is petite, immensely clever. Vain,
But sews. He, visibly, is no great brain.

Married in '52, in the Canal Zone.
Their windshield is a U.S. flag decal zone.

The NCO Club is their highest ridge.
They do not social climb. They play no bridge.

All day the pastel rains go freshly over;
Brilliant cannas take their beady cover.

Sundays, on the warm lanai, the funnies
Curtain-raise the sports. A choice of honeys

On a choice of breads, and, by the gallon,
Pineapple. Call it jaundiced watermelon.

Children join them. One is almost fair,
The other crippled, in a canvas chair.

Discussion. Pause. Then, looking in his cup,
The sergeant answers, yes, he will re-up.

On the Freeway

It has the strength of the seducing thought.
It is the road: one passion early taught,
One method once achieved and after sought.

Escape, the competence we soonest learn,
Abstractly beckons at the latest turn,
Confirming, "Rather travel than to burn."

Coiling seduction, thrust, St. Paul's own way,
The interchange coerces toward the Bay.
Behold the serpent, who devours the day.
Sun where the jaws divide, gold egg of prey,

Survive in us who are the shining back,
A little more than scales, if by some lack
A little less than knowledge. Be, warm sack

Of promise, all the life we shall not have:
The goldest, stillest fruit guile ever gave.
Clear future tangent on the western wave,

Blood sluggish where the off-ramp trumpets, nears,
We shed or straighten. As the rattle slurs
The patterns of the diamond disperse.
No other exit. Drive on who prefers.

The Corpses at Zinderneuf

From enemies become staunch liberals
We cordon yet the unimperiled walls—
The steadfast watch, its monument alike,
In whose *beau geste* empire forever falls.

Defected into stateless carrion,
We enter blindly (vizors over bone)
A Legion more than ours anonymous;
To be henceforward colony foregone:

A gestured death repeating without will
The bettered lessons of an alien skill.
Absence as presence; where, in skies not ours,
An empty flagstaff seeks the zenith still.

Phantoms

Assume the domino and be avenged;
And I for my part, immortality exchanged,

Must wear the mask of your disfigurement—
The shadows and the sewers where I find content,

An aging crossbones of the organ console.
You, purple now from skier's helmet to your insole,

Have Africa for your Palais Garnier:
Its armies Offenbach, its courts auto-da-fé.

Sit then in judgment, all your scarfaced years
And all your deprivation stopping-up your ears,

Lest you should hear in newfound glamour, plea
For pity that was never yours. To fire and flea

Commit my savages who look to more.
I then, high over crowded stalls and plush red floor,

Close under your forsaken, gaslit dome,
Where—haze—the nineteenth century has still a home,

Reeks still of those crude energies it burned,
And where the Best and Brightest, whored by what it earned,

Tonight act out their guilts—I, even I,
The patient skull, the long despised, put patience by:

On cop- or dropout, Peace Corps volunteer,
In vengeance of my own saw down the chandelier.

From *The Defense of*
the Sugar Islands

1979

The New Suit

The buttons may be brass; the serge is blue.
There in the mirror is the wearer you?

You did not order you a uniform.
Has then your tailor, acting on a firm

Conviction wish is truth, outfitted—seen—
That dapper mercenary you might have been?

The second mate spruced up to go ashore;
The pro on pass whose entourage is sure:

Mira, Soldado! Cheebee you my sister?
Muchacho, I have seen that fat disaster,

And the self who saw her breaks the spell.
Blue is for bellhops in a good hotel,

And brass . . . well, brass is one aspect of greening.
Mirror on the wall obscurely grinning,

Is not choice a fairest face of all?
Each apple beckons. Must one poison pall?

Ex-draftee, blitz your brass and square your tie.
Whoever lives, at your age, lives a lie.

Military Funeral

To bury these of whose far wars I was not part,
I bring a flashy livery, an unmoved heart.

I have white spats, white gloves; the rifles have white slings.
I have my mind unfailingly on other things,

As have the mourners. If their looks are not quite stares,
The flag that we shall fold and give is not quite theirs.

Korea and its rutted snows export them grief;
Cane sugar, fraud, per diem checks sustain them life.

Insistent in the mango trees, the sound of hours,
On yellow rot the brown bees feed. On plastic flowers,

G.I. insurance, funeral directors eat.
Viuda is not twenty. If our glances meet

She will invite the squad for coffee. I am bored;
I lift my dark sunglasses off. Now I have scored.

And, meanwhile, we have taken up our formal places.
Here, the reject of a cockfight pecks my laces.

On a signal I have raised my rifle high.
It has occurred to me that more than mangoes die.

The coffin falls, a squared-together Humpty-Dumpty.
My round of sky inside the sights is blue and empty.

From *Keys to Mayerling*

1983

Alternative Autobiographies

He retires after 34 years in the Canal Zone.

Mid-morning on the Tivoli veranda. Hours
To kill and then the plane. One more humidity
For, so to say, the road, a vapor part recall
Now rises off his coffee cup. Outside and in,
His dark sun shades fog over. Luckier in stocks
And wiser than his colleagues, he has kept up ties
Stateside. However, Phoenix and the trailer park
Are for the moment ashes, not rebirth. Not ease,
Nor ease from pain, nor any desert's clearest sky
Will compensate him for the overscoring haze
Of freighter smoke on this horizon, or that first
Salt taste of coffee as it clears the sweat of lips
In mornings sweetly, whitely damp. Not to come back.
Never to see again the great hibiscuses
Fed on the drip of air conditioners; or see,
In driving rain, the hull profiles rise in the locks
Like giant silhouettes from *Jane*. You, de Lesseps,
Where are you now we need you? In the petty suits,
The endless countersuits of your reviled old age,
What did you think of? Not the brokers, surely. Of
These cities, feverless? Or of a self still older,
Crying in delirium "Your life is there;
You have no other." Turn the sewers in the streets
And tear the nets to bind the buzzing wound within:
It is the sundered land itself that is the fever.

He is the last American in Johannesburg.

It was not you I stayed for, although if I stay
Hereafter it will be for you. It was for, how
To put it? Symmetry. A balance of the life
Within and world without, in wholly present time.
No past, no future. All the promise in the States
Or every wreck in Europe is not nearly worth
High summer on the Rand, our thunderstorm at four.
It's Boxing Day. Buy liquor and invite some friends
For when the lightning gathers. No experience
Like two drinks as it flashes sixty miles and back
From east to west to east, and on the balcony
Each thunderclap shakes down the ice cubes in their bucket,
At the very moment that a smell of dagga
(Always, twenty servants smoking on the roof)
Echoes the ozone. Racist? Jo'burg is no worse
Than elsewhere. That, of course, can still be rather bad.
The trouble will not start just yet. A little luck
And we can be here through July. One Winter more!
New Zealand's starry flag as the Republic's sky,
And where the Cross is rising, dark horizon bright,
Insurgent veld fires as a second zodiac.
The money is in Switzerland and we are here.
Have you another definition, Happiness?

Imaginary Sargents

I
Nellie Melba

Untitled—not that, Dame, she has not tried—
She wears, as Marguerite the pure of guile,
A coronet too like a duchess's
For happenstance. Her own pearls, hung in ropes
Down to her knees and like a negative
Of ermine tails, or ideal boomerang,
Perhaps account for want of interest
In Mephistopheles's jewel box.
Upon the straps of those high button shoes
Her velvet hints at, she will lift herself
To inlaid gates her necklace shames. The Trio,
As she sees it, is the Jewel Song
With wires. Who of us doubt her? Trill is will.
Faust, in the meanwhile, has his work cut out.
Except for Avarice and Social Climbing,
One a dangling purse and one a codpiece,
Who would dare seduce the Queen of Song?

II
Viscount Greystoke

Nothing of the jungle there; no wound,
And, as is customary with the Master,
No anatomy. Sun helmet, mount,
A polo mallet say activity,
But are such ikons as might fit the life
Of any peer. Of shipwreck and the ape
New jodhpurs do not speak. One all the same
Can see behind the viscount of the pose
The traveller of the vine, who, in a sense,
Is what she sees who has commissioned it.
If, as is far from inconceivable,
God's judgment on the artist were a life
Eternal and to do the cover art
For paperbacks, what should we have? A La
Of Opar in a triple rope of pearls
And on the cupped-out slab of sacrifice
An amateurish torso? Better that
Than have, in their own time, in Lilydale
Outside of Melbourne, some fifteen years on,
A rich old diva and her still young husband,
Sharing, in a life of bickering,
A coterie of vapid, ignorant,
Tone-deaf Australian homosexuals,
So far from Gounod and so near to theft.

III
Alfred Douglas

For reasons of his own the portraitist
Has given the etiolate a sun tan;
Has, of his effete material,
Produced Lord Jim: white suit, a wicker chair,
An eagerness to please. The point in common,
Vanity, profile puts off. At sea,
If one did not know better, one would say
Lord Alfred could be trusted utterly.
It is the highest flattery to know
Appearances deceive, and then deceive.
The worm is in the wicker, and the white
Of linen is the swath of Lazarus.

IV
J. Bruce Ismay

Of Tuan Jim the gross old age. The jump
Into the black and everlasting hole
Has left a weak, unwilling hermit, whom
Our painter, not a prophet usually,
Has shown us in advance. Unfortunate
How at the subject's side, upon its stand,
A model ship has shown to all the world
Its too few model lifeboats; how this canvas,
Painted for a Board Room, must be moved
At once to some far warehouse, there to wait
Until its copy, heading sunken stairs
And going green beneath a tripping sea,
Rise up to show to cowardice the dark,
Deep, unforgiving image of itself.

V
Mrs. Leland Stanford

A plainest Jane. In black brocade and four
Spit curls she is the goddess and machine
To all that she surveys: a brave new world,
Of sandstone courtyards and of red tile roofs.
If it is somehow Sidi-bel-Abbès
In Palo Alto, she is chaperon
Enough to keep the very Legion chaste,
And all Algeria besides. This paint,
However, cannot mock her, nor can we,
For all that earnestness, and let alone
The showing of it, is a true lost art.
Another portrait or another year,
And, like a king in tragedy, who treads
On purple to the axe behind the door,
In summer white, an old executrix
Must go to Honolulu to the cares,
The treacherous companions, and the draught
Of poison on the ship's night-table. You
Who know the guile, the spineless arrogance
Of both the world and the Academy,
How can you doubt that for their paradigms
And for their ease they had their conscience killed?

From *Hurricane Lamp*

1986

Do Not Judge by Appearances. Or Do.

The children of the crossing bear their sleep
Still with them, like another instrument
To weight them down; a shadow of the French horn,
Say; a heavy nimbus of the trombone.
Their cases miss the concrete of the walk
Exactly, as their noses the exact
Height of their turned-up collars. Now two more
Have joined them. Athletes, on the evidence
Of ditty bags and shoes, and wide awake.
The crossing guard is Ilse Koch, or if
She isn't ought to be: a leather cap
And body of a lampshade. Competent,
But not whom one would hire as sitter twice.
Will it be always their perception that,
Bold, safety wears the garb of violence?
Or will they learn in these too guarded streets
That pretty is as pretty does, but evil
May in fact be just as evil looks?
The final irresponsibility
Is never to impute, and all they know,
For now, is that the holster is a case
And what it holds is merely instrument,
No agent in the fight they fight. The trombone
Has attacked the ditty duo. Ilse,
In a world she both enjoys and knows,
Stops traffic and moves in to separate.

Why Fortune Is the Empress of the World

The insect born of royalty has Marx
And worker housing as a life; has sex
Or clover honey to his pleasure, as
Have we. The parrot speaks. All use: the ant
The aphid and the crocodile the bird.
What then is human wholly? Is it heart?
Fidelity exists in any dog.
Good Doctor who have found your Missing Link,
On your return what will you have him be?
Free agent or a tenant in a cage?

A simple test will serve. It more or less
Is this: can he be taught a game of chance?
It is not possible, you must agree,
To think of animals as gambling. Odds,
Except for us, do not exist. An ape
Assumes always his jump will reach the limb.
For all his skill, he cannot cut his loss.
We, on the other hand, at our most threatened
Turn instinctively . . . to Reason? No.
To Fortune, as a mindlessness of mind.
The random that we create creates us.
In overcrowded lifeboats, we draw lots.

Flying Friendly Skies

Our left and right show red and green: mute phonics.
A two-light Christmas in a sky of onyx,
The 1011 is an hour from Phoenix.

The cabin lights are off, and at my side
A sleeping Pfc., his waking bride,
Have heads an airline pillow may divide,

But only as a cut divides the cards—
In no essential. Having knitted yards,
My neighbor on the other side—her guard's

Up always—draws a game of solitaire.
"The point of Phoenix," says she, "is its *air*."
Sun City is for her the at, the where.

The two young people near the primal scene.
The solitary, tactful, has to screen
Her reading light. I? I fall in between.

A Dance Part Way around the Veau d'Or,
or,
Rich within the Dreams of Avarice

You poor, dependable, discreet small Mammon!
Had you form, what might it be? How summon

Arms of Moloch or the golden calf
If you are too exiguous by half?

A stripper's falsies, say? Transvestite's egret?
You are my dirty little open secret.

You prevent me, truth who act as sham,
From tribute as the worker that I am.

For gifts in childhood, my backhanded Baal,
Thank you. Your rebate let me countervail;

As in my busy, happy adolescence
You, the silent, stubborn, growing presence,

Sacrificed. I also thank you, center—
Part rather—of my being, for my winter

Each second year vacations. Cross I bear,
How I enjoy your stations! I, sole heir

Of that penurious young scare I was,
Gain now the ruby slippers. Eat cake, Oz.

Inflated quackery the tin ear praises,
Lionizer whom the lion dazes,

Ease the youth of whom you hit upon.
You are yourself what I now spit upon.

Income unearned, I say I'm quite above you.
In point of fact I love you, love you, love you.

The Garden and the Gods

Site of the world famous Easter sunrise service, the bizarre spines
and pinnacles have been ranked in degree of difficulty for climbers.
—A.A.A. paragraph on Colorado Springs

Field glasses on the cocktail terrace, I,
Rock climbers in my figure-eighted sky.

Long tenure, you, and if your handhold fails
Be where you fall (the figure eight avails)

Outside my field of vision. Why then watch?
To learn the look of what is mostly touch.

Practitioner that on the living rock
To your own ego nail yourself, no look

Of mine can teach you how to miss your thorns,
Or trust the nails, or move at last the stone.

The scrutiny that learns, its lenses hood,
And with it or without, well understood

For will triumphant, misconstrued as trust,
You equally are exhibitionist.

The coin runs out; dark shutters end your hour.
Ego, I have no nine-and-twenty more.

Out of this barren garden, then, to air
Whose gifts or whose embrace are not my care,

Go up in ignorance. As much informed
As mind's stigmatic purposes demand,

My feel for bleeding palms, for height will pass.
The cocktail and the cup, alike, will pass.

Pausing in the Climb

Sun on the cheekbone like a razor cut,
Vein at the temple pounding.
Brilliant in the altitude
Volcanic sand; a brilliant air surrounding.

And at the very barrier, the high
Vague cordon quarantining
Ether from the air below,
Shines out, as in the shrub's Mosaic burning,

A single thistle as a timberline.
It is the blood itself
Insistent on the edge of time;
The branching armature whose either half,

As in a scan, the prickling weed projects—
The one half red with air,
The other, tree of our defects,
Forever livid in the airless, near,

So formless blue. Unspeaking, burning blossom,
Crown upon the thorn,
Do beating heart within the bosom
And a clotting, cold inertia born

Beside it share one color, to invoke us
Future in a hush
Of purple? Will your image mock us
In the morning as a shaving brush?

The Strange Case of Dr. Jekyll and Dr. Jekyll

I drink no potion. To the double life
I bring no goatish hint of the exotic,
Have no weight of guilt to offer; have,
For now, no chilling drive of the fanatic.

My fleshpots—give them credit for perception—
Know me as the slummer that I am,
As I know them for their applied corruption.
What we are, to what we are we come,

And only too prepared to settle for it.
Commerce comforts, in these middle years,
Once one has learned the young do not abhor it.
Curious that hard cash and that sneers

Win out where youth and eagerness did not,
But wholeness in that age is antiseptic.
It is what one had instead of Hyde.
It also is the reason, not now cryptic,

That today I buy and do not plead.
Part capital, my cautious potion-sippers,
Wholly venture. There the surgeon's blade—
It cuts both ways—succeeds to Jack the Ripper's.

The New Dolores Leather Bar

> I adjure thee, respond from thine altars,
> Our Lady of Pain.
>
> —A. C. Swinburne

Not quite alone from night to night you'll find them.
Who need so many shackles to remind them
Must doubt that they are prisoners of love.

The leather creaks; studs shine; the chain mail jingles.
Shoulders act as other forms of bangles
In a taste where push has come to shove.

So far from hardhats and so near to Ziegfeld,
They, their costume, fail. Trees felled, each twig felled,
One sees the forest: Redneck Riding Hood's.

Does better-dear-to-eat-you drag, with basket,
Make the question moot? Go on and ask it.
Red, do you deliver, warm, the goods?

Or is the axle-grease, so butch an aura,
Underneath your nails in fact mascara?
Caution, lest your lie, your skin unscarred,

Profane these clanking precincts of the pain queen.
Numb with youth, an amateur procaine queen,
In the rite you lose the passage. Hard,

To know the hurt the knowledge. Command is late now,
Any offer master of your fate now.
You can, though won't, escape. Tarnishing whore,

So cheap your metal and so thin your armor,
Fifteen years will have you once more farmer.
Mammon values; earth and pain ignore.
Name your price and serve him well before.

Appalachia in Cincinnati

We who have bridged the river
Find our bridgehead comfortless:
A few square blocks forever;
Limits steel guitars express.

Beyond the surplus stores,
The pawnshops and the storefront missions,
Outer inner-cores,
Blacks pursue their own persuasions.

We, the heart of darkness,
From our beer-and-sawdust floors,
Look past the pavement slickness
Toward the rainy, sooty airs

Of lighted hills above.
You ever comfortable, your houses
Cantilevered wave
On wave above our poor successes,

Pull your drapes more tightly
Or descend from where you view,
Voyeurs, and do your slumming rightly.
Buy us breakfast. How

Exotic, here where necks
Are red and waitresses are minors,
Flannel lumberjackets,
Soulless food in all-night diners.

Occupied Ohio,
World that ends at Clifton Ridge,

World without end or I.O.
U. calls us from Suspension Bridge.

Watch with us one hour.
The second coffees cool, and, lucky,
We see wet skies clear.
Your sun comes to you from Kentucky.

Hunting

Deer season near the end; new boots
And red windbreaker for the red
Young man, who, sipping on a beer,
Hunts in the hardwoods, hound ahead,
Alert. It is, for all his gear
However, mistletoe he shoots.

Green as a serpent, in a sense
As deadly, shot off at its stem
The sought-for parasitic falls:
The Druid lure. Each in their time
Our sights are set for love, our halls
Hang out the call to violence.

U-24 Anchors off New Orleans

(1938)

The only major city, one would hope,
Below the level of a periscope.
An air so wet, a sewer-damp so ill,
One had as well be under water still.

The muddy river cakes us, camouflages.
Maddened goats, my crew go off in barges.
At a distance—I do not refer
To feet and inches—I go too. To err

Defines the deckhands; not to is the Bridge.
Discretion is the sex of privilege.
The streetcars meet the levee four abreast;
I cleverly have picked the noisiest.

A mad mapmaker made this master plan,
To wring out, of his grid of streets, a fan.
One German restaurant, well-meant but erring:
Ten kinds of shellfish, bouillabaisse, no herring.

Have my men fared better? Where they are
Becomes a high Weimar Republic bar.
There—lower Bourbonstrasse—lace and leather
Mingle in Louisiana weather.

Crack your whip, Old Harlot, pop your garter.
Who lives here is, by definition, martyr.
If I come back I'll think to pack libido.
For symbolism there will be torpedo.

Phaëthon

Unter den Linden

Of all the German-Greek
I only keep my chic.

The other gods, in ruin,
Have whatever Zion

Or whatever dusk
Old protocols may ask

Of elders. Youth and fire,
I harness my desire.

The quadriga whose freight
Holds down the Doric gate

I free to air. And beast
And god, to west from east

Lay down, without a name,
Divisive streets of flame.

All things that were, that are,
X-ray themselves and char:

Street lamps and corniced heights,
The lime trees' blazing lights

And black tall cinders. Day
Or wrath, I am the way,

The path. If I am truth,
Then deviance is youth.

Old order of our pains,
My Father, take the reins.

Berolina Démodée

Erich Mendelsohn's buildings on the Lehniner Platz are
presently occupied by a bowling alley and a supermarket.
—M. Henning-Schefold, *Frühe Moderne in Berlin*

City without shadows, hail!
Hail, *ville radieuse*. Yet, here,

something—haze, perhaps, soot on
high steel, my own middle age—

creates, as I stroll idly,
its illusion of shadow.

Rounded concrete, chrome, windows
that round corners, strip-windows

banding eave to façade . . . these,
here and there, like a darkness,

shade the bright glass curtain walls.
Did they once, in their far time,

seem promise of a more far
travel? I pass a spaceport;

I look away. At my age
one does not see without pain

Blitz Gordon on the check-out
stand of a fast food franchise,

in a building whose very
lines launch rockets. Dark *Moderne,*

suck back your shadow. Blitz and
I, we've turned a bit to stone.

Follower, we know you well.
You are the future grown old.

The Goblin Market,
or,
The Sorrows of Satan

The Southeastern Comic Book and Science Fiction Fair will
be held in Atlanta August 13–15.

—*Atlanta Gazette*

To bargain hopefully for dog-eared Marvels
Come a stutterer of twenty-nine,
A deaf mute ten. And if the flesh has evils,
Here, in the epic sweep of sword and pen,

Are not the extra syllables subtracted
So the silences can add a tongue?
Ur-hero in whose image, much collected,
These your servants are not made, among

Your *Ur*-er, more heroic acts, give up
For once omnipotence, the role of prompter;
Deign to know, yourself, the unmoved lip.
Consider: if I promise, I your tempter,

All the world and tights that never crease,
How will you answer dumb, get thee behind me.
You will not? Well, if you need to ease
Clay feet, I shoe them. You know where to find me.

Meanwhile, be that speech of last appeal
To trade for whom the barterers must come.
The stutterer can say "Adida deal";
The mute lips move, around the chewing gum.

Imputations

The poppy carries into time
Its squalid link with opium,
The rose its colors of the wars.
Who, on the brokers' trading floors
Has seen a tulip frenzy? Debt,
Greed, speculation blossom yet,
And in the waxen bud not one
Suggests itself. The frenzy's done;
If in the morning light the look
Hints still at bubble, if it broke
It would not bankrupt, only say
Enthusiasms have their day.
The morning turban, wide, noon crown,
Quick tangibles, go up and down,
As though mild breezes studied trends,
So our instruction were their ends—
A Dow Botanical, where bronze
Is up, gold down, and either warns:
No totem wholly without tribe;
No value some will not ascribe.

Page from a Bar Guide

In glassy ice, erect
And formal and exact
As any Christmas tree,
The juniper, *esprit*
Inviolate and form
Confined, has prisms, Norm,
Freak, diagram, its spines
Convert the sleet to tines.

And, blue of ice on blue
Of berry, fast accrue
The cedar flavors, taste
Of freeze. They do not haste,
Our days of Gibsons, roses,
But they come, whose spruce
Is in glass still. November's
June; the gin remembers.

The Aswan Rowing Club

Above the dam the Nile at pool
Sits idle, and below that dam
It idles too. Cool afternoon
And the insistent *accents graves*
Of the feluccas give alone
A sense of movement. From a small,
Moderne construction on the shore,
Incongruous, but no more so
Than stereo on minarets,
Move out to break our brilliant still
The Aswan Crew: in their lean shell
Congruity of stroke, of time,
Of place, for all their hint of Cam.
The megaphone is not a drum,
But oars are oars, and in their beat,
In little, are the galley, slave,
The distant sweats of Actium.
Muezzin, coxswain, local crew,
The triumph you enact is you.

Eniwetok Mon Amour

> Yerkes Primate Center has a population of laboratory animals exposed to atomic radiation in the nuclear tests the military conducted in the 1950s, an experimental resource that could no longer be assembled.
>
> —*Annual Report*

The lab technician is an entrail reader
Late to own it; science a restraint
That cages for us future on the hoof—
Curt life forms that will mutate and will speak,
Or that will keep their peace and reassure.
Already, in the nations of the cage,
Destruction gathers or does not: the ape
Grows old uncancerous, and if he dies
Outwits us, as he has no issue. Flies,
For all we know, have bred the danger out
Long since, and are our fruit's destructive heirs.
High priesthood of the Pyrex and the knives,
For whom the seed of seeds, unstable still,
Is ripening to law, do not suppose,
If in the flesh irradiated, seared,
You find the image of the branching cloud,
It was not there before. The tree of blood,
The twisted prophecy you cut toward, is,
Unlikely augurers, not yet response;
Not the accusing, unambiguous
Mutation that you seek. It is the norm,
And what it says is: monster or to be,
For each if not for all, for flesh that waits,
The future is by definition monstrous.

Scheherazade in South Dakota

Mitchell (1312 alt.) is located in the James River Valley, and is widely known for its Corn Palace, the only one of its kind in the world. Entirely decorated in corn and products of corn, the exotic-appearing structure was erected in 1921. The Corn Palace each year attracts thousands of visitors from South Dakota and neighboring states.

—Federal Writers' Project, *South Dakota, a Guide*

Implacablest, remotest, levelest!
Immensest prairie, out of what false East

Have you created, dome and corn and spire,
The world of Rimsky-Korsakov entire?

Ill-mated as the nightingale and rose
The brick of Main Street and the *quelque chose*

It partners: all too visible Kitezh,
A Rimsky bauble, bead, and Bangladesh,

Or silent Baghdad of the elder Fairbanks.
Have shops, haphazard banks and doctrinaire banks

Financed it, or (have chickens change of sex?)
Did it their cockerel lay golden eggs?

It is that gleam that to the farm snow-maiden
Poses fresh careers as go-go maiden.

In the small town still it is a wind
That says "O wondrous land, O land of Ind."

The wind is gone; a whirlwind here and there
Clocks off the dusty time of one more year.

On Sindbad of the storefront time lies heavy.
Rimsky was a young man in the Navy.

Via Spaceship through Saskatchewan

Another planet, or the look thereof:
High prairie featureless, high clouds aloof.

Above the summer air the arching frost;
In every breeze some hint of winter lost,

Of cold to come. Two seasons spread at once,
One sky whose quarters all are north, no tense

You negate dulls our flashing heaven, fights
Its mounting charges that will be the lights.

Invisible aurora, heavy wheat,
This other Saturn knows its ring is sleet.

And, cities of that planet's cautious plain,
The clustered silos elevate the grain.

At the Mercy of the Queen-Empress
(Victoria, B.C.)

Two grasses by the Empress hedge;
The one to smoke, the one to edge.

I lean a while upon the edger,
Smoke a joint, add up the ledger.

One week now I'm twenty-eight.
If I go home I'm not draft bait;

I'm not young either. Edgar Hoover,
All the smarts are in Vancouver.

Why did I come here? That town
I left was brown on brown, on brown;

So misted trees and sunny water
For a while did sort of matter,

Like the sunlit summer nights,
The great green dome outlined in lights.

It's summer over; statue viewing
Shows the Queen can stand renewing.

Summer's done; B.C., R.I.—
Whichever, Vic, it's soon goodbye.

You tourists on the morning ferry,
Hot tea cosies rest you merry.

You're that picture in the shops:
Rowboat and rower, stand-up corpse.

Don't look for lights; don't look for tinsel.
All ashore for Toteninsel.

Ghosts

To Galveston among the oleanders
Mrs. Alving comes with Pastor Manders.

So transported from its fogs and fjords
Can fate grip? Do they hold, the silver cords?

Male nurse around the clock; a handsome trust fund.
She is valiant. It will be a just fund.

Here, also, some justice is. A heat
By 8 A.M. enough to drive out quite

Whatever glides among the local headlines;
Eager fury, unaware of bloodlines,

Stegomyia all the night. Yet, too,
Such mercies as has fifty. "I and you,

Hélène; our coffee made with chicory;
Palmetto fans, in their poor mockery

Of breezes."
                    "You and I, the Alving money;
Porch with, how to say, a Suck-the-?"
                                                    "Honey-

suckle vine. Put out the lamp, Frau Captain,
And come to bed." On shutters, swags, nets slept in,

The great mosquitoes light. But for the nonce
The furies wait; the lamp is in its sconce.

The Miller

Without imagination, but with long,
    Sure knowledge
I release the arms and set the sails.

He, heir of reading much and meaning well,
    To tillage
Alien and to the soil unknown,

Climbs on his mare. The wind turns back his charge;
    A servant
Waits always to blunt the folly's edge.

It is incompetence the future hails:
    Gaunt, antic.
I, meanwhile, grind the grain and feed two fools.

A Distant View of the Chinese Wall

Alien navigators whose deep space
Is dark behind you, bold automata
Who focus randomly whatever disc,
Whatever grid you have for telescope,
How will you, orbs, interpret these: an asp
Of stone by day, a graph of sparks by night.

Out there in your eternal present, probe,
You must well realize the wall you see
Is of a past the burdened light transports.
Can you envision, cores, incurious
Investigators of a nearest void,
The crowded time of garrison and fires?

Of raging signals heaped up one by one
To urge our message toward the towers east,
Old wars the moving dots across your screen?
Know you the nomads of the isohyet?
How the wall defines it, and the rain
Obtains no more beyond? Adventurer,

Eye who exist in helmet or in head,
Lens, do you come, as sentry everlasting,
To identify with all who watch?
Or where you see a planet gone to dunes
Stretch west of Kiayukwan, the jade last gate,
To land and be as alien as they?

News for Loch Ness

> The Great Salt Lake is at its highest level in sixty years,
> and threatens surrounding territories.
>
> —AP

A golden angel, rigid in the lifeless water,
Trumpets silently, green deeps his judgment come.
Salt, more and more an architect, a water Goth,
To all the Temple's major pinnacles adds minor,
Benchmarks when the Lake is Bonneville again.
Down to the triple spires, that glitter in the grains,
Equipment of the treasure seekers drops and lights.
Long pikes break in the crusted doors: the veil is rent.
Nowhere the vessels; robes are not, nor any gold.
Faith hid them in the granite mountain, with the names.
Outside the orbit of the diving helmets, name
Without a genealogy and life for salt,
Leviathan engenders: "Bonnie," of the Lake
Its legend guardian, a symbiont of gulls.
The trumpet sounds; salt moves; the giant tail sweeps by.
And, effigies in leaking shrouds, iron masks, torn tubes,
A marriage of air, the plunderers lie sealed.

The Chinaberry Tree

Its shape uncertain in the bloom that scrims it,
Purple, and itself a haze of gnats,
The tree that will be knowledge, or what seems it,
Beckons in the rising heat and waits.

Its shade will feather, and be serpent: there,
Instinct to take the field and meet the beast,
Are bound, already bargainers, a pair
On whom the subtleties will all be lost.

The altered apple, as if randomly,
Exerts its blunt appeal, and though who fall
Acquire a taste, it is not learning. Try,
Avenger, angel posted, as you will,

The sword that flames exile shows up to be
Dessert stuck on a skewer, and the taint
Of Adam, late and early, gluttony.
How tartly, as the sandflies learn, the faint,

Soft blossoms harden in their unmeant Eden
Toward the green, emetic berry: scent
Nil, outline clear—late come-on for a want
Too uninformative to seem forbidden.

Seeking a Level

Omnipresent in the Hanging Gardens
    Falling water.
Stair of stairs and vine of vines, a stream,

A sound, descends the stepping blood: Euphrates
    Raised to heaven
To become the ditches of the tiers.

The morning cataract pours off its cornice;
    Noon has dried it;
In the afternoon the lower basins

Shine with amber of a sand accruing.
    Now, in the evening,
Climbing as the setbacks one by one

Scale off to darkness and the upper courses
    Soar in sunlight,
Come the gardeners to light the lamps.

Leaf, wick, leaf. Fire, the final fruit, breaks open,
    Upward cluster
Weightless at the cotton of its stem.

The newest, nearest leaves in pairs are parching;
    In the siphons,
Soon, the muddy artery renewing.

Is it the highest terrace that is greenest?
    Or, fed with time,
The roots at bottom where the water falls?

Hurricane Lamp

In warm cut-glass the geometric fire:
Triangle the half or diamond the whole,
Unstable in the still the bright parts pair,
Vibrate, divide; as if to say the gale

Engenders in the eye, and in the wind
Are lapses where the fire can tower high.
New smoker of a charcoal filter, mind
You do not burn your fingers as you try,

Face lowered toward the bar, to suck the flame.
In vortices as calm, ineptness wrecks;
In proper lighters, in the wettest storm,
The hooded flint rolls sparks along the thumb.

Here, have a match. Its height two hands protect.

Our Lady's Juggler

The miracle is mine, My Lady.
Do not think your lifted hand,
Your so late simper count. The steady,
Prompted poise of no hoops in the hand

And some hoops in the air surpasses.
This I make for you of rest,
Eye, wrist—a going magic—grace's
Access neither harms nor much assists.

Grace is to have no need of grace,
And I who send out no prospectus,
Leave no memory, give phase
To fall, in giving mass my little ictus.

In the Kingdom of Jerusalem

Secular heirs of spirit's little hour,
We govern in the aftermath of frenzy:
Ordered watches where the Crusade ends.
Between the Dead Sea and the live, our narrow,
Alien land. We signal, and the torch
Is for the shore levant, as its response
Is for the desert fastness the decline—
Two fires our width, our panic, our defense.
Who guard the shrines, add terraces for grapes,
Exploit the pilgrim, wed the infidel . . .
They (we) back up against the evening star.
Near Hesper, newest bulwark out of Europe,
Flash from shore to sand the flickered strength.
As, when the flood recedes, the salt is structure,
We, fore retrospects of brimstone fall,
By margin castles pillar-up the dawn,
Who glisten by the fact of shrinkage. Heap,
Rear Guard, the brazier high; and if from star
Nor West no answer comes, assess your creed.
The zeal that brought you here must buy you off.

Adding Rattles

The season turns, and to its chillest blood
Bears witness that a skin must soon be shed:
The rounding self forsaken: with its scars,
Its old concealments worn to use, be lost
Also our shining tread that knows the earth.
Another year of clarities and shade
Demands its other dazzle to conceal,
And on our backs the diamonds are fresh.
Old Belly, can you learn again the ways
Effaced? And you, Blood each time more enclosed,
Can you account it, in so hard rebirth,
All gain that you should see beside you, stiff
In death and in this wisest light transparent,
What you were? Who gain here otherwise
(Warm!) no envelopment not still to lose,
And one more sound to warn each touch away.

So Here It Is at Last

News, boredom, debt, guile. All are borne, but all are crosses.
How to be a man of fifty cutting losses
   In the loss of nerve.

How very long ago, in simple confidence,
One took the day at hand as what would issue thence,
   And as the just desert

Of act and its own past. Vague future, quick to come
And sure to disappoint the shape you shadow, numb
   Your coming with the sting,

The thrust of change: each hope you monster, year abort,
A nothing in our non-response—the drugged retort,
   The undistinguished thing.

The Alfano Ending

At the request of Toscanini and of Puccini's heirs, Alfano completed the unfinished third act of that composer's *Turandot*.

—*Grove's Dictionary of Music and Musicians*

Of that other person who began,
I have the work, to do with as I can.

All his imagined endings left undone
I must imagine and reduce to one,

That necessarily will be despised,
As even I know how the realized

Falls short of the potential. Instant mask
And lifelong cruelties I have the task

Of making viable. I see it out;
One earlier could leave the end in doubt.

You challenges I now would most avoid—
My given and my lack—the past deployed,

So intricately flight is either met.
Each riddle, Princess, has one answer: *stet*.

Therefore I do my mechanistic best
By love in which I have no interest.

Of hints and sketches, scenes scored long ago,
I fashion might-have-been and make it go.

A younger man (O time and time to spare!)
Set down these elements that are my care.

The grafted life I give another's say
Is no late masterpiece. But it will play.

Promises, Promises

The rain was real, that in the lashing water
Leaves its white unease, its easy spatter.
Neither truth nor force nor pitted glitter,

Fraud, the double rainbow gates and gates
Its high wet distance. Arch of violet,
Vague outer arch in which you bright are set,

The hope you portal is the air you are:
As little firm, as unparticular.
Faint colors general and nothing ours,

To each as each his end must here be sold.
The rain was real; be you a lie well told:
Air's seven-colored bridge from gold to gold.

From *Between the Chains*

1991

Persistence of Memory

What is it that a string around the finger says?
    Remember? No,
Remember to remember. It is Fool's Regress,

Our little act of distancing that, ruse enough,
    Will bring up front
Such dark and backward as we otherwise repress,

Once tedium begins to do the work of time.
    Trash, payments, locks,
Abysses all; and, worse, birthdays in middle age.

No fool forgets to order lobster, chill champagne.
    Might that occur
His aide-mémoire had better be a cordon rouge.

For double duty, heavy duty, handcuffs serve—
    After the fact.
The chains of masochism prompt. Is it the mind?

And if they come, hospital or the gallows, like
    Detail to crowd
Then wholly to estrange the one detail our life,

Mnemonics at the end will bring it flooding back.
    Around the arm
The bracelet with the dose: around the neck the noose.

Hedy Lamarr and a Chocolate Bar

Showings are six a day, continuous.
No need to wait in line or be on time;
In any case the plot will be generic:
Boy meets. Scorning the concession stand
(I am austere, for not much more than twelve),
Unfed by choice I go to meet the dark.
Algiers a frame or two before the end,
And in her big close-up Gaby departs,
Rogue Helen at the railing of a ship,
To wreck the blood as on the wall of Troy.
It is a vision that transfixes. Gel,
Dead center in the aisle, I cannot move
So long as ecstasy stares out ahead.
The vision vanishes, and Charles Boyer
Comes on to suffer who cares what. By now
I am so shaken that I turn around,
Retrace my steps, and thank the taste of Mars.
If, showings later, I become aware
That my experience is every man's,
And every man, if *she* is on the screen,
Is rooted in the aisle as I was, too
Exanimate to stumble toward a seat,
It does not mean that under Mitterrand
I womanize. And at our age who wants
Algeria. But I know what I know.
I have seen beauty stop men in their tracks.

Prometheus in Polynesia

The beachboys douse the flambeaux; at the tideline it is dark.
Log drums—contemporary, but no matter—thunder out
Abstractions of the storm and heartbeat, surf outside the reef,
Heights' very sound of seismic fire. As if the drum were god,
Force creates of itself a flesh full grown: a wisdom male,
Not of the forehead but the fingertips. His two batons
Ablaze at either end, a dancer leaps in light he mocks.
You could not possibly explain to him what hubris is.
If fire is of the air, not theft but gift; is of the rock
Inside the crater as it reddens, he who masters it
Is not a prisoner, not priest. He is a twirler. Change
His sex and there is something of a tassel dancer there.
Drum major in a lava-lava, puppeteer whose strings,
Whose puppets are the fire, he is not quite invisible,
Nor would he wish to be: footlights he juggles in his hands.
Whose is revenge? If any vengeance gnaws his liver out
It's that of rum. Not, though, just yet. A torso's fabled ease
Reminds us that the will and vision of the primitive
Can be taught nothing by the stroboscope. The torch outspeeds
Its own blaze. Orbit of our vanity, the fire goes free.
In figure eights the orange salamander bites its tail.
Full circles smooth and feather. In their going, coming flame
The dancer freezes in his postures speed makes visible.
Greek fool, fool of the Renaissance who huddle by the lamp,
If lava grips who uses it, it is no eagle's claw.
It is an Oversoul in pleasure taking back its own.

When in Doubt, Remain in Doubt

Not even on the eve of Salamis
Did Delphi give a competent response.
No oracle does, ever. That is why
Great men consult them. Oracles are doubt
Objectified, but left ambiguous,
So as to force a choice. In scrap-iron pomp
And strength of China's gold, the Emperor,
In mid-November 1941,
Has entrails made of plastic summoned, quick
To tell him "Let the punishment befit
The crime." And so the secret task force sails.
Commanders Short and Kimmel, one might add,
Did not consult, not even one another.
May of 1945. As Saul
Sought out the Witch of Endor, in a smoke
Filled room in Kansas City Harry Truman
Hears exotic dancers speak in tongues.
The meaning is not clear, but just may be
"Waste not, want not," of which one must assume
H. heard the first fourth only, as he wastes
Hiroshima and Nagasaki. Some,
Including me, do not do oracles,
But we aren't great. And of the cities two
It's Nagasaki I should like to see,
For reasons having not to do with bombs
But with Puccini. *Trust in wooden walls*.
It's they which have the best acoustics, Del;
And if the Persians come (Iranians),
Or have the bomb, is stone more sheltering?

Acid Rain on Sherwood Forest

The longbow, one would say, is natural;
Is an appropriate technology.
The crossbow is the downward path to Krupp.
It has a trigger, eyepiece; has a stock
Firearms have learned from. One would say. One would,
However, be quite wrong, as Baron Krupp
Might point out. Compound bows are anything
But natural, as they are laminate,
And what is natural about a graft?
We have, as usual, let sentiment
Define the natural. Our sympathies
Are not with progress but with Robin Hood,
Who is himself mere envy wearing tights.
What has redistribution of the wealth
To do with archery? It was the Krupps
Who had the world's first pension plan, and built
Its first real worker housing. Had *sick leave?*
We cannot speculate what was the life
Of Merry Men grown old. The arrow flies,
An infantry's or Time's, and how the wound
Arrives is of no consequence. Had Cain
No weapons but his hands he would be Cain,
And Abel dead of strangulation. Child
Of nature, little boy of five or six,
Why have you pulled the rubber suction cup
From off your arrow and begun to sharpen it?

Bank Notes

Parnassian in its simplicity of greed,
The Banque de l'Indo-Chine, obdured in privilege,
A presence on the distant side of two world wars
And two republics, looks increasingly to be,
Of their and our more recent wars, a clear first cause.
If Indochina in the 30s is a lost
Atlantis, it is Aristotle's, not Plato's,
In that the vision and the ruin most submerged
Is its Prime Mover. Out of undertows profound
But all too scrutable—come at the beckoning
Of justice and of so much blood—the Bank appears.
It is in mint condition, having been the Mint,
Or Bureau of Engraving at the very least.
Its currency, as the Depression deepens, holds
Its value, having never been exchangeable
For that of France, and keeping to a specie rate
When France devalues. As immediate result,
Hanoi and Saigon have the most expensive shops
In Europe or in Asia, and the fewest sales,
As rubber and as sugar will not sell abroad,
And planters have no money. Cruise ships give wide berth;
Angkor gives in to bats it is the color of.
No crash concerns the Bank, whose chief activities
Are lobbying in Paris, kept up on a scale
That would embarrass de Lesseps in Panama,
And speculating in Shanghai. The Privilege,
Renewed for five and twenty years in '22,
Protects it absolutely from the Bank of France,
No model of responsibility itself,
But not an international mah-jong concern.
Vichy both understand at once. The Japanese
Do not disturb them, knowing that it was the banks

Who pressured Vichy to admit them. As they stage
For Luzon and for Singapore, the Bank calls due
Its notes on Royal Dutch and the Batavia
Exchange, another background noise imperiling
Pearl Harbor. Policy and war much isolate
A colony that serves two masters warily,
But not to the extent the high exchange rate did.
Behind that silver barrier, at their own speed,
Away from Western eyes, a thousand opiates
Grow strong; and poppies, red however, are not red
Without companionship. The sugar in the fields
Rots into rum; the rubber dies above the graft.
The private Bank has never skipped a dividend.
On schedule, monsoon rains sweep warm and colorless
Across the Saigon River into New Saigon.
Inane canaries droop on concrete balconies.
Hats, hollow in the crown, deluge and cool the hair,
Protect the eyes in wide straw circles from the wet.
Tricycle wheels make grayish egrets in the street.
It rains in gray side streets as never in the heart.
A continent . . . subcontinent? . . . side continent
Once more is going under. There is this to say
Of it and of its Bank whose creature from the first
It was: it moved its funds from where its mouth had been.
So many decades later, did the U.S.A.?

Correction and Amplification

> *Boudin,* the dark, unbelievably hot sausage beloved of the
> Legionnaires, is unknown outside North Africa.
>
> —Charles E. Mercer, *Legion of Strangers*

High stumps that were the palm trees are the lights;
The low palmettos fence the stadium.
The High School football team of Lafayette,
Louisiana, runs out on the field
In contact lenses and an endless text
Of Cajun names. It is the Catholic
High School; a jewelry of crosses tics
Among the cheering section and the band,
Whose majorettes are Vietnamese. A priest—
Ex-chaplain, or of some sophistication—
Sees to it that the pom-pom is confined
To two cheerleaders, who are blond and male.
The buzzing mildness of the winter night
Is all we have of Indochina; that,
And rattling in the unbeheaded palms.
Sahara is the stronger presence felt,
Although the locals have no sense of it.
Although the caps are not the képi quite,
It's

     Hot Boudin! Cold Coosh-Coosh!
     Lafayette Our Savior! Push! Push! Push!

The south of I-10 vowels make the rhyme,
And couscous here is cornbread. Boudin, though,
Is Boudin, even if it's made with pork,
And with the pig's unspeakables at that.
Our Savior's opposition does not flinch.
A little of the march-or-die is there,
As well it might be. That opposing team
Is Algiers High. Algiers, Louisiana,

Opposite downtown New Orleans.
But post-colonial is where you look,
And if the march sounds French, all marches do.
Take back the pom-pom, Girls; Algiers, rip up
The infidel and make that next first down.

The Marquis de Lafayette knew revolution too.

Inducted

Socialist realism paints the "Tax of Blood"
As Herod at the slaughter of the innocents,
Vast Turks impaling Christian children on their swords,
Ravishing mothers, tearing infants off the breast,
And, in the middle distance, torching granaries.
The burning grain fields are of course a scene generic,
Useful equally for World Wars I and II,
Teutonic Knights at Novgorod, the Japanese
About to starve Port Arthur. As to why these Turks
Should care to burn the possibility of tribute,
Art does not comment. Outside the gallery
Marxism of a local form has done its work
Attractively. The town is bright and circumspect,
If, by the river, obviously Ottoman.
It is provincial irreducibly, its youth,
Unlike the youth of Belgrade, innocent of jeans.
In pairs and trios they carve tree trunks and are bored.
Admit it, tractor artist: neither I nor you
Can carve a true initial in a local wood,
As much as small towns bore us. Take an alias.
Imagine you are me imagining the scene.
Our small wistaria adds blue drops to the water;
In its fragrance, gaunt, a Turkish officer,
Itinerant draft board of one, is offered çay
Upon a table-tray. Drawn up in front of him,
Four adolescents and their father. "Tell me which,"
In Bulgar says the Moslem. "I need only one."
"The eldest has good teeth," the father volunteers.
Oedipal conflicts do not have their only site
In Macedonia, the which the officer
Is quite aware, if not exactly in those terms.
That sibling staircase, notes he, has one riser missing.

Is he hidden in a cave, the favorite?
"We do not bite our foe. What of the cloven chin?"
"Left-handed, and the younger knows the tongue of sheep.
I need him for the flocks."

                    "And at the best of times
You farmers have one son right-handed out of three.
Choose. Let the ambidextrous pick among themselves."
He well knows who the pick will be; the cleft of chin
Has winked two times at him, and with his either eye.
"Should you consult your other brother?" says the Turk.

        . . .

A last hill edging all the golden hills of Thrace,
And past it, for a gaunt recruiter and his troop,
Rise up the ruin of the Land Wall like a scarp,
And like the letters of an unknown alphabet
The minarets and domes lined on the Golden Horn.
A gypsy by the gate is dancing with some bears;
A sherbet seller, massive pitcher on his back
Is bowing double, to defer, or start the flow.
It will be thirty years before the new recruit,
The new initiate, allows his home a thought,
And he will think then of the blue wistaria
That in the water sheds its days toward Istanbul,
And counts the days of youth, in whom the tax of blood,
So irresistible, is paid and overpaid.

Berlin-to-Baghdad

(Constantinople, 1876)

The rail construction nears Seraglio Point,
And where the beach, already narrow, ends
Below the harem seawall, German care
Decides to send a diver down. If piers
Are necessary, one must sample cores.
The diver, in his complicated suit
That, as the helmet meets it, might well seem
Doubt's rubber janissary uniform,
Iron turban, dips into the Bosporus,
A non-Leander of a cautious firm.
The double current, where the Marmara
Runs on the bottom warmly north, and where
On top of it Medea's wild Black Sea
Pours south, disorients him in its chop,
But on the bottom there is blue and peace,
And there is horror. In his first surprise
He inadvertently bites off his air,
And only when his jaw relaxes frees
His intake valve to breathe. In front of him,
As if enormous tulips sprouted heads,
A score of women, sewn-up to the neck
In weighted canvas bags, and with their hair
Threading the current as it steadies, move
From side to side like Humpty-Dumpstresses.
He jerks a rope to be drawn up; he knows,
As he ascends, the garden he has seen
Is truer image of the Straits, and heart,
Than Sestos or Abydos, and that he,
And all his crewmen, and the sultanate
Of all the world have each in their own way
Numbered, bagged, and tossed. The Lorelei
So many times repeated there below is small revenge.
Assistants help him screw his helmet off;
He turns it over and is sick in it.

Immurings

The land walls of Byzantium, the Maginot
Line of their time, and that time was a thousand years,
Expressways parallel today and on-ramps breach.
The highways, frankly, have the more impressive scale,
And certainly are more an obstacle, as in
Berlin the structures for the viewing of the Wall
Exceed the Wall. The Wall of China is at least
As cogent as it ever was, which is not very.
Say it is a sort of contour line gone wrong,
And may well cease beyond its last hill in the view.
The wall of walls, the self-enclosing self-enclosed—
Great serpent, seamless mouth, broad bitten tail of stone—
Is Cartagena of the Indies, whose main gate
Is tower for a clock, as if to say that time
Besieges always; is the sieging-engine, brute,
By whose monotony the first defenses crack,
And is the treachery by which a culture falls.
It is the matrix out of which technology
Is catapulted, and the cauldron out of which
The napalm and the Greek Fire pour. Not that a wall
As concept can be superseded. Cells have walls,
In brains as well as prisons. Thought and speech, at base,
Themselves are barriers, or could not be defined.
The final barrier, mere space, is absolute
And is at hand: the universe's end is hid;
The words upon this page a single space divides.
Ex-space, dry moats in Istanbul are garden plots;
The tunnels in the Maginot deep truffle runs.

Power Failure

In Parktown in Johannesburg,
Along the season-facing ridge,
The mansions of the Randlords fall to time;

Or, too granitic to destroy,
Defy the clinics, fast-foods, shops.
In this one, grandly, Thomas Cullinan,

For whom the diamond is named,
Converted carats into brick,
Or pyramided common on preferred.

In that one, co-conspirators
Are rumored to have planned, if planned
Is not too strong a word, the Jameson Raid.

In all of them, on summer days,
Wide-open windows suck the dust;
The lightning flashes as the current fails.

On dark terrazzo, cubic hail
Keeps up a dice game. At their back
And out of sight beyond the vacant mines,

In other thunder, shining tin,
The vast Southwestern Townships—East
Los Angeles strung out along the Rand—

Go bright, one streetlight to a block.
The one-eye hot plates heat the meals;
In Parktown, as the hail rounds into rain,

High candelabra light the trays,
High teapots shape the lightning flash.
The grid is not so blown it will not fuse;
The evening not so charged it will not clear.

Between the Chains

Brokers and their clients and hangers-on would congregate
in the short section of Simmonds Street between Market
and Commissioner Streets. The Mining Commissioner had
posts erected and chains hung between them in order to
close the area. Hence the "open air Stock Market" and the
phrase "Between the chains."

—John R. Shorten, *The Johannesburg Saga*

It neither shames us nor is gain,
The broker's cry from chain to chain.

It is the human urge to trade,
Our standoff with the urge to aid.

If by it bleeding hearts are wrecked
I am not; you aren't. Nor was Brecht.

Up, Mahagonny in the claims,
And dig. Life has a digging's aims.

Here is the only city built
On neither trade nor sand nor silt

But on the rock itself of gold.
It is not, it will not be, old.

It holds much guilt, some hope, all pains,
Between the chains, between the chains.

R.U.R. or Are You Aren't?

The miners huddle in their rising cage,
A self-consolidating other. Small
Stockholders whom Anglo-American
Is eager to impress, we foreign four
Observe a changing of the shifts. It may
Be barbarous, but no one on the Rand
Supposes gold to have become a relic.
I can read my fellow goldbug's mind.
Having observed, correctly, that the streets
It drove us through are Lang's *Metropolis*,
The Company, she hopes, employs robots.
She is our mover of initiatives.
A scissor gate squeaks open; checking-off,
Lang's White mine captain gathers-in the lamps.
We shall have now the robot *Trauermarsch*.
Or shall we? At the very "point in time"
That shower and a whisky cross my mind,
I notice in their golddust-blasted eyes,
Beyond the utter weariness of bone,
A look I know, a lifting of the chin.
I too have drunk what is genteelly known
As Bantu beer; I know the tactile quick
That as one peels it off is boots and socks.
(How late the Board Room limo comes to call!)
Our Lady of the *République* Weimar,
I deconstruct you. Theirs a look I know,
You know. It is the sun below the yardarm,
Signaling the day may yet be saved.

Apocalypse as Genre

The air blows full of gold dust, and Johannesburg
Its false redoubt
Is glorious in the detritus of the mines:

A Bible city glittering across its storm,
Its salt and sand,
As if the lightning granulated and the wind

Were bright particulates. It is a Phantom sky,
Not nature. Jet
Trails are not clouds attenuated, chariots

Not sun. God did not make the metal but the ore;
And flint, not fire.
Creation did not end upon the Seventh Day.

The artificial skyscape of the fighter planes,
The cyanide-
Imbued sand barrens, diggings, mock-Chaldean towers,

Owe nothing to the Garden and do not repent.
Belshazzar's gates
Stand open and his diamonds spill out the vault.

"Prophet of Doom" is optimist tautology.
Who foresees good?
Look back instead on Joshua, on Daniel.

Coerce the sun, command your time, confront the flame.
Transcending tribe,
Embrace the fire-brick, wreck the damper, tread the ash.

The feast, the writing, and the wall go on and on,
So long as what
Waits in the balance is not nature. Art can cheat.

I could construct you, of these elements at hand,
A brand new Ur,
A fasting Babylon. I offer you the Rand.

Some People Have No Small Talk

From isolation to the dart board, a trajectory
Of social distance, barroom Concorde replicas have aim
And fly. Who throw them, having failed to replicate so much
As a synthetic self, enjoy, or settle for, a least
Companionship the game provides. It comes, conclusively,
To this kind fact: the lowest score is not quite nothing. Darts,
Intended or at random, on the mark or off the wall,
Make good the arc and are a concord: link forged beyond sound.

Campion in Uniform

Error predates computer error. Quite
Through manual incompetence alone,
Our mess-hall has received a year's supply
Of Queen Anne cherries. Breakfast, lunch, at break
Or in the field, we dine on Royal Anne.
The thought is still enough to make one gag.
God did not mean His cherries to be white.

The gag reaction is most fiercely high
In years when lipstick, fashion says, is pale.
In Basic Training, if one thought of lips,
It was in terms of maraschino red.
Most Stuarts, dropsical or dull and gross,
Missed great careers as warrant officers.
Ripe, cherry ripe, what can a Queen Anne cry?

For the Scrapbook of Mrs. Charles Black

Columbia, South Carolina, in October,
1952. The iron palmetto, symbol
Of a symbol, arms the lawn, the statehouse steps,
Somewhat as if the Krupps had turned to gardening,
Or Vulcan left behind a giant swizzle stick.
But what to swizzle? In a suicide revenge
On servicemen, downtown is dry. Intense research,
However, presently reveals there is a bar—
It seats four—lost in the Columbia Hotel.
Two drinks are legal. Not, you understand, two drinks
Per person. Two *kinds*. One can have a champagne cocktail,
Sugar cube and all, or have a Shirley Temple.
How, pray, can an adult man, in uniform,
Unman himself by ordering a Heidi-Ho
In public? Try the U.S.O., and lukewarm beer?
No, anything but other servicemen. And, for
The moment, I am not in public. I'm alone.
"I'll have a champagne cocktail." May a draftee's curse
Turn into ash and iron the garden clubs and gardens
Of this ladies' luncheon town. Cheers.

                                     Enter now,
Internal exile written on their faces, she
Who past all doubt was the outstanding shot putt star
Of Carolina High, and the Platonic, fixed
Idea of a failed interior designer.
"Wet a cube, Ray. Soldier, I spent every night
From first grade through the fifth in curlers. Hell, fie met
Ole Shirley Temple Agar on the street today
I'd snatch the silly bitch baldheaded. Name's Faye Head.
I do interiors. And here's Du-ane DeWitt.
He drives a truck." It's as it should be, Halloween;
I've found a home.

A soldier's blessing, Duane and Faye,
From somewhere in the Caribbean, in the future,
Where the bars are legion and the gardens Eden.
In your desert, as a memory of me,
I pray you get blind drunk. Piss on the iron palmetto.

Mainstreaming

Fort Jackson in the twilight and the coal smoke
Oddly looks like San Francisco, Tank Hill
Being Nob Hill and the mess-hall steps
I sit on any hill that overlooks.
Un-Californian in the extreme,
E Company goes smartly by, then G.
Night training in the field, presumably,
And odds are it's their final. In two weeks
The training cycle ends. I have a scale
Of orders cut that goes from one to ten:
Korea's minus eight; Presidio
Is ten. "And here the Moron Legion comes."
Above me and behind, Mess Sergeant Fay;
And who refers—his slur is literal—
To Able Company, whose Draft Boards have,
In manic zeal to put down Minus Eight,
Inducted borderline retardees. Not
To mince words, Able drools a lot. "Nine weeks
Of Basic," says the Sergeant, "and they still
Can't mitre sheets." A bit self-satisfied,
In broken step they march the asphalt streets
As if they crossed a frail suspension bridge.
I have no way of knowing, but I see
A Turk Street of the future: vile fatigues
And leather strapped on in the strangest spots.
A look that later age will know as stoned.
It is their cadre whom I notice most;
As if they each one had a shoeshine boy,
A valet, private barber. And a sylph
Who wipes their lips with Kleenex if they drool.

. . .

"If they discharge them then they have to pay.
Hospital, pensions. So experiment.
It's monkey see and hope that monkey does.
Two-thirds of 'them', one-third of 'us.' Of course,
If they fuck up then we are punished too.
Ten weeks and none of us has had a pass.
Don't ask me what my sex life may become."
My confidant is Connor Kennington,
With whom I went to high school. We've an hour
Or so of freedom, in the Service Club.
The Tank Hill Service Club. The Nashville Sound
Is occupation army in our own.
"I'm in the ranks to spite my family.
I write them that I shower with idiots
And they write back 'But are they White or Black?'"
"That Field First Sergeant's not an idiot."
"Ed Crowley? Yes he is. He had it made
And threw it over. He was acey-deucey
With the Provost Marshal."

                    "AC-DC,
Connor."

              How would I know? I'm a normal.
I'm the one-third. I can make my bed."
"And lie in it?"

                "I sleep with idiots."
"But are they White or Black?"

                   "Shut up, you mother."

          . . .

Now I sleep with idiots. With two,
End-up on either side of me, in traction,
In the Base Hospital. I've ptomaine,
But I'm improving. They are burned and blind,
And who could teach them Braille? An accident,
I am informed, last month on the grenade range.

Connor never disappoints. First orders
Cut for Honolulu in a year.
He came by Sunday for a goodbye gloat.
"Pulled out the ring and stuck it up his nose.
Blew up these two, the range instructor, Ed,
Himself, and six observers from Taiwan.
Aloha. Don't let bubbles in your drip."
I walk him down the hall, and at the turn
We meet a tall young father with a child
Swung on his either crutch. The empty leg
Of his pajama has been neatly pinned,
But crutches are an instant shabbiness.
"O.K., you two. Let Daddy learn to walk.
Edwina, reach me up a Kleenex, please.
The tricky part is how to blow my nose."
The children giggle; Connor is all eyes.
"*That* is a family man? I'm not surprised
The Marshal threw him out. M. P. indeed!
Who trusts a man that won't make up his mind?"
"Well, if he takes him back he'll save on spats."

. . .

Civilian for thirty years or more,
I'm sometimes in the City. In a dusk
Of smoke and traffic, for a second time
Today, my cable car has stalled. In frank
Defeat I sit down on its wooden steps.
Nabobs, how near your hill is, and how far.
Hotels and barracks, idiots and grips,
Nob Hill ahead is grown Tank Hill behind.
A trolley bus, the thinking man's transport,
Rescues us, urging by its postered sides
That one support Brain Damage. Thank you no.
I hear the voice of Connor Kennington,
Echoing, as it were, from Waikiki.

"Ought to be stuck in jars at birth, dumb blobs."
And no doubt, Connor, many of them are.
Tomorrow will be better. Rent a car,
I think, and drive through the Presidio.

Fin de Siècle

*The political history of much of the Third World is One
Man, One Vote, once.*

—*Rand Daily Mail*

Southampton, Bremerhaven, Antwerp . . . No parades
And portholes sealed, hospital ships in guarded docks
Onload: the walking skeletons, quicklime in crocks,
Pets, stretcher cases, eight month pregnant chambermaids.
The nineteenth century is having none of AIDS.

Balfour has died of it; the Household Cavalry
Has been reduced by half. On Flanders waterfronts
It has become "Congo Revenge," and Berlin hints,
In heaping up its pyres, at "Pox Britannica."
Fence wire enough to rim our five main continents

Is bound already for the flats of New South Wales;
In Tanganyika, craters will become reserves.
The flag of quarantine, above the world's wide wharves,
Is flying ever yellower. No ship that sails,
Save only these, has certain port. Drug shipments, mails,

Coal, diplomatic bags themselves, wait on the ramps.
Surviving public-school boys go in stowaway;
Archbishops of the Church of England almost pray.
There will be hearts that bleed, transvestites of the lamps,
And very little concentration in the camps.

Will there be greed, and courage in the face of death?
Be for the blind warm steadies, hearers for the dumb?
Be scarred young men whose minds are not on vengeance? Some.
A self served, whole, the century goes out in wrath.
But its decisiveness has saved the twentieth.

The way of presentism is to whore the past
For passions of the moment. That is pestilence
Also. If there are cures, unthreatened lives long hence,
Then what I write is *Masque of the Red Death* at best.
If not, I am the One Good Man in Sodom, once.

Publicans and Sinners

The beach hotel is no house built on sand.
    It is on coral.
The house on rock—at least, that which will stand—
Is Simmons' Lounge. Which would you say, offhand,
    Is more immoral:

Social climbing (my hotel), or slumming?
    At Buddy Simmons'
B-girls at the bar are up and summing;
Pentecostals wait the Second Coming.
    Till its summons

All persuasions present have their price,
    As have innkeepers.
Bright green casino felt or grubby dice,
The difference, at last, is imprecise.
I've money I can burn. I need a vice.
    Assault day-trippers?

Franchises

Ezekiel the Prophet dealt in wheels
Within wheels. He did not, one must assume,
Derive a living from it. In this cave
Of chromium, whose walls are disc and wire
And spoke, expertly, Hubcap Annie does.
He is a mild young man whom prophecy
Would not become. You give him year and make,
And option. He will go unerringly
To where that model is. His modest fee
Includes the installation. Like a test
Of knees the rubber hammer swings down twice.
His stocks as yet unsorted chrome the yard.
A fence's fence? Well, let us say Ann takes
His wheels on faith, as did Ezekiel.

Texarkana

Two city halls, and—how it irks—
Two mayors, each with perks.

The jail in Arkansas is small.
In Texas it is tall,

But barely adequate to house
Such cowboys as carouse.

The men back East, that is to say
A hundred feet away,

Have quiet vices, or have none.
Not ever known for fun,

The East is, here as elsewhere, dead,
Dull, dry, and no doubt Red.

Well that State Line Street divides
One town that has two sides

And shows two faces. Has Berlin,
In that split it is in,

Division any more complete?
The checkpoints here, discreet,

Invisible, are, like the Wall,
Not psychological

But surface tension: water, oil.
Not severance: recoil.

Knowledge Is Power,
But Only If You Misuse It

Telepathy does not exist,
And for sufficient reasons: one,
It soon would make society
Impossible, and two, its cheap
Bypass, in circumventing speech,
Would make sex all too possible,
Which is to iterate again,
It would destroy society.
A fortune-teller's crystal ball
Is blank correctly. Were it not
What need could she have still to work?
No ESP would waste its time
At second-guessing packs of cards,
Unless, of course, the tests were held
In meaningful environments,
That is to say, casinos. Heads
Telepathy will never pierce
Revolver bullets will, and prove
Roulette is Russian, guess is risk.
Whirl, Chamber, whirl! And what is Chance,
That it should make the world go round?
Outside the fragile skull or in,
A future read, our past divined,
More knowledge does not turn the trick.
It is deceit that does: drive wheel
Inside of Fortune's. Cheat who read
The palm so soon of silver shorn,
You know how far to read the mind.

Retouching Walker Evans

Every photo—every, every one—
From the Depression having now been found
And anguished over and become the stuff
Of coffee-table books, I see go by
As in an M.G.M. parade of gowns
The bony women in their all but rags.
And on her Shelby, Mississippi, porch,
Reviewing stand of the originals,
My great-aunt Lela, dead for forty years,
Is present as an absent frontispiece.
She is a seamstress some few years retired,
Whose reputation and whose marginal
Prosperity are owed to a device,
Her own, for making over-bosomy,
Notoriously over-bosomy,
Deep Delta women look less so. Her trick:
Bolero-like effects—diagonals
Across the diaphragm and diamonds
Below the arms. A steel dressmaker's eye,
As they head townward on a Saturday,
Takes in the trucks and White sharecroppers' wives,
Who, flat beyond the dreams of any mode,
Contrive to nurse. Each is a gauntlet thrown;
A challenge, as to write backhandedly
Might be for an accomplished forger. And,
Having repeated a bolero theme
As often as Ravel—that other seamstress—
Nature's nemesis now finds herself
Imagining a bertha. Desperate,
But who has seen such gauntness heretofore?
A rival reads her mind. "All right, how *would*
You fill them out?"

"A sort of Empire waist
And heavy gathers at the collarbone.
That's all you can do. Short of feeding them."

· · ·

Between the coffee-table poverty
And now, the first decade to intervene,
The Forties, brings to military wives
Discreet per-diem checks, and to the steel
Eye, trips, nostalgia trips, in the bright form
Of certain Metro musicals. Queued up
For one of these, she is exchanging views
With an exhausted woman who could be,
A few pounds heavier (in Anaheim
The Okies are becoming prosperous
And being hateful to Hispanics) she
Who in the Thirties challenged expertise:
The K.K.K. madonna of the truck.
That expertise a poster now offends.
"Pure, flat-out desperation. In that last one
Even stiff boleros didn't work.
And look at this thing: organdy rosettes
Stuck on her clavicle. Has she no shame?
It's like believing you can call away
Attention from potatoes with a pea.
Of course, in her case nothing *can* be done,
Except for breast-reduction surgery.
If I were head designer do you think
I'd let them put my name on trash like that?"
"Them colors ain't much either," says a voice
In which an expertise may also speak.
"She's Remnant Counter pink and feedsack rose."

Other Directed

Two roads diverge, each in a yellow smog.
It is the Freeway. I? I take the one
Most traveled by. It makes no difference,
Nor should it. Eight wide lanes and well-marked turns
Will get you there, without the waste and mud,
Ornate delays of detours. If you know—
Mind, really know—so late itinerant,
Where you are going, is there, now and then,
Some reason not to take the easy way?

Method

The tom-tom in the jungle thomases
Its message; on a mesa in the rear
The signal smokes. Respectively they say
"I'm standing here and beating on this drum."
"I've lit a bonfire: now I blanket it."
Beyond the blunt, beyond the obvious,
What is it possible to say? Is code
Even conceivable in languages
Which are not written? Is the changing beat
Mnemonic? Onomatopoeia? Or—
A parlor-game password—key pre-arranged?
Does fire uninterrupted also speak?
How, tribal poet of the flint and drum
(And your intelligence, I am aware,
Is not inferior to mine) . . . how, bard,
In symbols would you like to have to say
What, at this moment, on this page, this says?

One of the Boys,
or,
Nothing Sad about My Captains

As bellies at the bar, and heads unbowed, unbloodied,
Drink up as men of means the boys I understudied.

No academic has a right to sneer at you, Ducks.
If forced to choose I think I'd pick an honest Ku Klux.

One needs at seventeen a passing public manner.
Mine was no urge to raise a mast, or nail a banner.

The in-group tricks of this crowd were enough. They served me.
They may, from certain traps, uniquely have preserved me.

You cannot know, subcultures, artists, mixed assortments,
How *you* may have to learn the tongue of trust departments.

All you who garner fresh rejection slips, or lack mail
Altogether, do you write from sheer self-blackmail?

All sports intensely bore me, if they are not bloody.
The Country Club, however, is a richest study.

I scorn, from my guest vantage, nervous, job, class tensions.
The steady and the whole are my preferred dimensions.

One cannot say my erstwhile cues, my captain models,
Shine like stars. They certainly were not my idols.

Still, they had their moments. Less is more. And "I,"
That inner self whose effort was to slip it by,

Undoubtedly they see. The Bridge must type and rank you.
The inner me on view? He's doing nicely, thank you.

Links

My young grandfather, for the me of four,
Blew smoke rings. I, these long years more,

Without much gift, can, nonetheless,
Redeem my breath from utter shapelessness.

I have no grandsons, having had no sons.
Still, it is good to know that as he once

Made fire his speech and bridged a clinging void,
However differently employed,

I sometimes smoke a little too,
And might bring off the tricks he used to do.

Open Wounds

One test infallible, one only measure
  Of a loss that never passes:
    Ask the loser
Does he think of it when he must shave.

Of lovers I've cast off I think at leisure;
  Of my enemies (those asses).
    You, my razor
Brings me—you the burn and why I shave.

The morning blade, a masochist's small pleasure,
  Puts my tortures in their classes.
    None the wiser
I, and time no styptic aftershave.

Laying It on the Line

How does a heart of stone
write a love poem?
In free verse, of course,
to show how little rigid
he really is.

I was in love with you
a long time;
I am still.
It calls for no change,
obviously, having been itself
the very "wax lost" that fixed.

You might
want to know, or might
not, that just for you,
just once, I broke my meter.
Such is, as you care
to look at it,
my casual admission of wreck,
or noble Roman
equivalent of opening my veins.
But as you see, the beat keeps coming back.

Epilogue

He Whom Ye Seek

As neatly ordered as a mortuary wall
For undersized Hispanic nuns, or battery
Of drawers for the mummies, narrow shouldered all,
Who were the victims of thalidomide, rise high

The safe deposit boxes. At this distant bank
I have been stashing in for nearly fifty years
Are found a birth certificate, in fading ink;
Gold watches two grandfathers left me; lavalieres

Nobody ever wore—I hope; the orange shares
Green superseded as reverse stock splits occurred;
My Army discharge; passports; wedding rings in pairs;
A diamond I brought home from Johannesburg.

I storm the vault today to add to that long hoard
These master copies of my poems, which I roll
And stuff among the silver. Moth and dust and sword
Will not strike here. My young trust officer, a droll

Expression on his face, has learned yet one more hope
On which his customers place value. Hail, farewell!
The double locks go shut; I insecurely grope,
In pocketing keys, to see my ticket is there still.

I have a plane to catch. And as the stone was rolled
To validate the sepulcher, the round steel door
Engages. Although much amused, the Bank's enthralled
Head keeper of the gate, whose father I saw floor

A bouncer once, is surely as dependable
As any bonded guard or tomb archangel. What,

Possessions being curses but possession still
Nine points of law, to any who investigate

Can he my trusty angel say? "He is not here?"
He is, however. He is every single share,
Knife, fork, and spoon. I am the blood the portraits were,
Those carats, iambs, trips. All of my life is there.

Wall, coffins, keys, was it a stunting or a growth?
It was the risk of so much safety. It was both.